THE BEST COLLEGE STUDENT SURVIVAL GUIDE EVER WRITTEN

The one book <u>all</u> students should own before starting or finishing their college experience

MJ WILSON

Foreword and research by

JONATAYE PRATHER, PhD

ISBN:1482021943
ISBN-13:9781482021943

DEDICATION

This book is dedicated to:

The dreamer. The believer. The hopeful.

The one who wants more.

To all of you who just need that extra push or encouragement.

For those who have had enough of "What if" or "I should have" or "Can I?"

To those of you who wanted a sign … Something to guide you.

Someone to say, "I believe in you."

Yes, this book is for *you*.

So forget about what your parents did (or didn't do).

Forget about where you were born or where you live now.

Forget about all of those who have failed before you.

It's YOUR turn now.

Show us who you really are. Show us how it's done.

And show me that college diploma when you finish!

Anyone can go to college. But this book is dedicated to those who finish.

In other words, it's dedicated to YOU!

Don't let me down.

-MJ Wilson

CONTENTS

FOREWORD

If you think getting great grades in high school and scoring well on college entrance exams means you're guaranteed success in college, you are destined to fail.

The Researcher – My name is JoNataye Prather. I am an educational consultant, college professor and doctor. As a multiple graduate of The Ohio State University, I earned my most recent degree (PhD) in 2010. I'm currently a college professor at Ohio Dominican University in Columbus, OH, and frequent conference speaker on the subject of "non-academic barriers to learning" – a topic very dear to my heart. I've consulted with students and teachers in urban and suburban schools concerning this topic, written a dissertation about it as part of my doctoral program, and presented my research at national conferences about the effects these barriers are having on student academic achievement, as well as college retention issues.

The Problem – As an educator for more than 15 years and considered a "double minority" by the world we live in (female and African-American), I know *full well* the struggles students face during their college experience. I have witnessed many students' successes and failures throughout my career, and in doing so, have noticed one glaring, obvious "red flag": **the success of today's college students is rarely due to their academic prowess, but rather, their ability to cope with and respond appropriately to the non-academic barriers that often keep many of them from graduating.**

In other words, it's not how smart students are, it's how well they handle or "survive" these aspects of college life:
- homesickness
- making friends
- joining on-campus clubs
- getting along with their professors
- the demand of balancing athletics, work and school
- participating in risky behaviors like sex, drugs or alcohol

- campus parties
- studying for exams

You may think this kind of stuff is minor in comparison to academic problems, but research shows otherwise.

The Solution – After meeting MJ Wilson for the first time in 2008, I learned of his experience with non-academic barriers, how he dealt with them successfully, and his desire to share his solutions with the world. It was then that *I felt compelled to partner with him,* add my research to his experience, and finally address this problem. Now, for the first time in my academic journey, I can honestly say I feel comfortable endorsing a book that creatively, passionately and enthusiastically not only discusses these non-academic barriers to graduation that so many students face, but also the retention challenges many universities contend with as well.

The Author – *MJ Wilson is by far the best educator I've ever met.* With more than 15 years' experience of educating, inspiring and motivating K-12 and college students himself, he is certainly a master in his field. The way he commands a classroom, earns the respect of his students and inspires his colleagues ... the man is nothing short of an amazing teacher. One of my favorite qualities about him (and this book) is that he "keeps it real" by providing *practical advice and real-life stories* (the kind students love to read and can *actually* apply to their own lives!) Throughout this book, he inspires and instructs students to thrive and maximize their collegiate experience with easy-to-implement tools that help students succeed not only academically and professionally, but also in life, long after graduation.

The Charge – Your college years should be the *best* years of your life, positioning you to have a successful future! MJ Wilson and I have written this book for you to help make that happen. Use it properly, and you'll not only attend college, but you'll also graduate AND dominate while you're there.

-JoNataye Prather, PhD

7

Introduction
The Hidden Courses You *Must* Pass!

If I Only Knew Back Then What I Know Now

You are sooo lucky! What I have laced throughout these pages are the stories, the memories, the heartaches, the failures, the victories, the passion, and most importantly, the guidance ... the guidance you'll need not only to survive college, but in some instances, *life*. The guidance I wish someone woulda[1] shared with me. The guidance that cost me thousands of dollars, countless tears, sleepless nights, and seemingly endless study sessions.

What you have in this book is a collection of the life experiences of myself and others, along with examples of what worked for us and what did not. What you have is what we were missing: a roadmap of how to start, where to begin, what to avoid, whom to follow, and how to get there. A plan with the end in mind.

> **Regardless of your current position in school, this book will be advantageous to you.**

Whether you're reading this as a **HIGH SCHOOL JUNIOR** or **SENIOR**, or

---

[1] In this book, I could write "the correct way" and use big words and fancy language. However, I've decided to write just as I speak, giving you my true authentic voice. Rather than getting someone who's trying to impress you, you're getting ME ... someone who's trying to be *real* with you.

8

FRESHMAN in college for the first time, you'll desperately need the clever tactics and basic information that so many new students are never taught, but still learn, unfortunately, the hard way. Adhering to the principles in this book will greatly increase your chances of surviving college and not only graduating, but graduating *on time*.

If you're returning for your **SOPHOMORE** year, this book will guide you and keep you from making the mistakes that so many sophomores normally make, now that they're no longer the "new kid on the block." Mistakes like transferring to another school when they should've stayed right where they were. Or changing majors only to change them again ... and again ... and again. These mistakes are *costly* and can be avoided if you have the right plan.

If you're a **JUNIOR**, this book can keep you from falling for the lure of "big money" and a new job offer that's offered a little too soon. Such offers often knock juniors out of the race for their college degree altogether, or simply delay their graduation date another two or three years unnecessarily. It can also keep you from suffering from the insignificance so many juniors feel after attending school for three years (or more) and not really "owning" any of it. This lack of ownership increases school apathy, which increases your odds of not finishing, thus causing so many students to quit when they are sooo close to the Finish Line.

And finally, if you're a **SENIOR**, this book will confirm some of the choices you've already made and improve your overall college experience with a few "tricks of the trade" while also inspiring you to leave your mark or legacy before your grand exit. You don't wanna graduate and find that there were so many things that you coulda done had you only known. You can learn how to exit in grand fashion and have something to add to your resume so that you'll stand out among your fellow graduates when you enter the job market.

Whatever your collegiate level, this book is of great value to you. I highly recommend that all sections be read, studied, and learned. Yes, *all* sections. If I had the information I'm about to give to you when I was your age (or at least in your position), my life would've taken a much better course. Some of it I knew then. Most of it I learned later. But you ... you're getting it all in one shot, in one book, at one time. And as the saying goes, "When much is given, much is required."

Now About Those Courses ...

When you read the title of this introduction, you may have thought that the hidden courses that you must pass were referring to actual college courses. You know ... like English Composition, Algebra, or Economics. But those are not the types of courses I'm referring to. What I'm talking about are the unwritten, unguided and unknown courses that aren't graded by a professor, but rather, by life itself.

These courses determine how you perform in your *actual* college courses. They aren't hard to pass but they *can* be complex or even difficult if you aren't prepared for them. So that's where I come in. I'm here to guide you through these normally unguided courses and see you through your college experience successfully. (Lucky you!)

Although the hidden courses I've mentioned above may go by several names, the names I've picked (which are stated within the chapter titles) represent the unguided, untold "rules" that so easily define so many college students' college experience. Some of these courses may seem easy to you, but make no mistake about them, they're *all* to be taken seriously.

As we go through this book together, I will instruct you on each of these courses, advising you on exactly what you need to do to avoid the pitfalls that exist within each of them, as well as helping you to make the most of them while you're in them.

I've also included a "My Solution" section at the end of each course as a way of allowing you to "pass" these courses successfully. **So please realize you are not alone in this!** You can go to college and graduate and I will help.

Without A Vision, The Students Perish
When I was younger my mother used to always tell me, "Without a vision, the people perish" and it's always stuck in my head. So here I am writing you about getting a vision, and I'm thinking of that phrase. Obviously, I'm not actually suggesting that you'll perish, but perhaps without a vision, your college career will. So let's look into this, shall we?

Coming up is a section with a box labeled, "My College Graduation Vision." This vision (your vision) will help you begin to see exactly just what it is you are setting out to do and when you should expect to have it done.

And it's very important that you complete it.

Please, don't be like me when I was your age (or in your position) ... I would see forms and questionnaires like this in books and pamphlets and think to myself, "I don't need to do all that. *I got this*. It's not that big of a deal." And now, here I am years later realizing the only thing I had was a bad attitude and a know-it-all mindset. Both of which cost me extra yearS in school (notice I placed a capital "S" on the word "year" to emphasize that it is plural, as in more than one year!) and THOUSANDS of dollars more than necessary just to earn a degree I could've actually been paid to obtain!

So don't be like I was! *Please* … complete the vision box.

My College Graduation Vision

Full Name

_____

I will start (or started) college in
_____/_____.

(Month)   *(Year)*

I will graduate from college in
_____/_____.

(Month)   *(Year)*

I will earn a G.P.A. of _____ or higher during my college career (or from this day forward).

I will not let anyone or anything take this vision away from me. I WILL make it a reality. I WILL do whatever it takes. I WON'T QUIT!

Signed _____

Today's Date _____/_____/_____

I know, I know ... You're thinking, "That's it? *That's* the vision? Shouldn't it be more in-depth than that?" Well, that's my point. Making your vision plain and understandable really is *that* simple. It's the part about making it come true that seems to get everyone all tangled up (it's not enough to see it, you have to take action!) And that's where we'll spend the majority of this book ... keeping you from getting all tangled up, and helping you take action.

For now, just realize your vision doesn't have to be difficult, it just needs to be seen. ☺

The Interior Decorator

Now that you've completed your vision box (completely!) be sure to go to my website (MJ-Wilson.com) and download another copy to place on your fridge, bedroom wall or bathroom mirror. (And don't worry, the form is free!) Just be sure to put it somewhere that you know you'll see it on a daily basis. Having your vision made plain (understandable) and put in front of you daily (where you can see it, read it, and believe it!) will remind you of what you're doing, why you're doing it, and where you're headed. (Think of it like directions to an event you want to attend in the near future, and focus on the clearest path to get there, in the most efficient amount of time possible.)

And please, allow me to stress this one more time: it's not enough to see it ... you **have to take action** to achieve it! You *must* turn your vision into action!

Hold Up, Wait A Minute ...

Perhaps you didn't complete the vision box because you didn't wanna write in your new book? If so, I'm gonna need you to change all that. If you truly, *truly* want my help, you're gonna have to trust me and follow my lead. So please, overcome that part of you that says you're not supposed to write in your books, and please write in this one![2] Not just in the sections made for it, but all through it! Take notes. Write in the margins. Highlight important ideas and concepts that really stand out to you. Then keep this book and review it throughout your college experience (at least at the beginning of each semester) to ensure you are staying on track. Each time you do you can skim through it quickly by reviewing and studying the areas you've marked that really "speak" to you and your personal situation. Cool? Cool.

Now that all of that is outta the way, whattaya say we get started?

---

[2] Reading this in e-book fashion? Great! You can still make necessary notes and highlights as your device will allow. You can also go to my website and download many of the forms and templates you find throughout this book for free, to give yourself something you can truly leave your mark on. ☺

Chapter 1
The First Month of School

So here you are in a new town with new friends and new teachers and new ... well, everything! So many things are new right now that there is actually more new in your life than old. It's an exciting, strange, and sometimes difficult time for many college students and often brings many questions to mind.

Should I change my ways to fit in? Should I keep myself and my ways and just be the way I've always been? If I do change, how much is too much? What about my religious beliefs, my music, my hobbies, my food, my talk, my study habits, my routines? Can I date or hang out with people totally different from what I'm used to? If I don't do what everyone on campus is doing will I be an outcast? Do I change a little, a lot, or not at all? Am I the only one feeling this way? UGH!

You Weren't The First, You Won't Be The Last
Let me be the first to tell you that you are definitely NOT the only person to ever feel the pressure about wanting or needing to fit in, yet not wanting to compromise who you are, where you're from or what you believe.

> *One of the beautiful things about college is that it allows students to somewhat start their lives all over again with a clean slate.*

Going to a new school full of new friends in a new town (or even an old one) can give all students a chance to "re-invent" themselves and start building a new reputation and life. As great as this opportunity is, it also comes with its own discipline. What I mean is, although you can start all over again with your life, reputation, style, etc., there is still a "template," if you will, of what is expected of you as a student. This template isn't written in the rulebook or as any student guidelines. These are unwritten rules that college life will often place upon you (knowingly or not), pressuring you to do or become something that otherwise you may not even consider doing or becoming.

The degree of pressure these rules place upon you depends upon the level of seriousness that such things are honored or expected on your campus.

For instance, if you attend a religious school, you may be expected to live according to a socially acceptable code of ethics within the world of that particular institution. What is not acceptable on your campus may be perfectly acceptable (or even celebrated) on another. If you attend a public school that's heavy on sports, you may be expected to participate in games, pep rallies and other functions that other schools may not even have.

Whatever the case, the most dominant groups on campus, or at the minimum, the most dominant groups that exist within the world you will be a part of during your college experience, will be the ones affecting you the most.

Now please realize, *the dominating ideals that these groups share or enforce are not necessarily upheld or shared by the college itself.*

Oftentimes, the college in which the group exists may even be opposed to such ideals held by its own on-campus groups. Other times these groups themselves are unaware they're even enforcing or pressuring people to adhere to them. Sometimes it's been a way of life (or "campus culture") for so long that it goes unnoticed by the majority of the students and staff on campus. Either way, these ideals and beliefs do exist (in some schools much more than others) and depending upon the type of school you attend (religious, public, private, etc.), you will be encouraged or discouraged to uphold them.

The Five Common Senses

The following is a list of some of the most basic ideals, beliefs and expectations that many campus groups and personalities enforce, whether directly or indirectly upon their members, and whether they mean to (on purpose) or not (without realizing it). You figure these out and you win! Well, not exactly, but you're definitely increasing your chances of winning, or in this case, graduating!

To help guide you through, I've added "My Two Cents" about each to let you know what I think or feel about these topics:

1. **Dating and Social Status** – Some campus groups may expect you to date or associate with only a certain type or "caliber" of person.

14

Such groups may have high expectations and demands of their members.

For example, a strict religious or private school with very specific expectations and its own code of ethics may not want you to associate or date someone with an opposing belief system or philosophy. Committing to be a part of their group (the school's) may draw an indirect expectation for you to not be a part of another. Or a school that's heavy on appearance and wealth may not favor the likes of your less fortunate friends and your posting of online photos and party pics with them.

However, what one group on one campus does with or expects from its members may have nothing to do with what a similar group on another campus does with or expects from their members.

Just remember, the rules that govern such groups usually include "unwritten rules": rules that aren't directly stated, but are indirectly expected and enforced. *And that doesn't mean that such rules are necessarily bad*, but it does mean that you will want to know what these unwritten rules are before totally committing to them or the group enforcing them.

Some groups may prohibit dating or affiliating with anyone outside of their circle for fear it may be seen as a negative mark on their social status and yours. However, other groups won't care who you hang out with, date, or whether you date at all as long as you attend their functions and pay your dues.

My Two Cents
- Whether you do or do not agree with dating or social status stipulations is up to you.

- If you join a group that enforces "dating rules" or "association rules" while in college, please realize that the people you place and accept into your world are *your* choice. They're the people you'll need to go to if and when times get tough. So choose wisely.

- If you're fine with the rules your group has given you, then fine. Join the club. But if you don't like the rules your group has given you or the choices they offer you, then maybe your

15

campus group isn't for you (and that's okay). Something to think about.

2. **<u>Religious Beliefs and Parties</u>** – Some campus groups will assume that you are (or will become) a "party animal" with no regard for your religious beliefs, dating practices, or even alcoholic tendencies (let alone how you'll feel the next morning). Others will expect you to follow a strict code of conduct, possibly even denying any involvement in such activities whatsoever. Still others may require your attendance at a prayer meeting twice a week, while another on-campus group with an opposing viewpoint may actually meet twice a week just to protest the very thing your group is praying about!

(College life can often be a microcosm of the world … Isn't it great?)

Whatever the case may be…

> *Religious beliefs and partying are two heavily debated and pressured ideals that many college students struggle with throughout their college experience.*

However, if handled properly, either ideal can be a positive experience within your college career and one that you look back on with great pride and memories.

At the same time, if these ideals are ignored or dealt with improperly, either one of them can make the conflict between the two so difficult that your overall college experience can be affected in a very negative way.

Enter Sheena, Stage Right

I'm reminded of Sheena, a girl I met years ago. When Sheena was in high school, she had a very guarded, conservative lifestyle. When it came time for Sheena to go to college, her mother sent her to a very conservative college with strict rules and expectations concerning what students could or could not do in their spare time. (This college had a no alcohol policy, a curfew for students, and a mandatory chapel attendance.) Sheena's mom did this in hopes that it would "keep my daughter safe" as she put it.

Well, Sheena went … And Sheena struggled with her foundational beliefs and her new found friends … And Sheena partied like a rockstar … And Sheena got expelled.

Listen to me. Your college isn't there to "parent" you. *It's there to educate you.* Get these wires crossed and you may find yourself right back at home where you started, paying for an education you never received and suffering from a mark on your resume you don't want.

My Two Cents

- As with the dating and social status, whether you do or do not agree with the stipulations and expectations of these on-campus groups and others is up to you. It's certainly not my choice to decide what you believe or protest, partake of or adhere to.

- You are now considered an adult, and although you may be "mothered" still by those at home or peer-pressured by those at school, at the end of your college experience, <u>you are the one who has to live with the choices you've made and the consequences (good or bad) that come with them.</u> So again, choose wisely.

- I don't recommend you just throw off all that you know or believe simply just to please someone else (like Sheena did). *What got you this far in life got you this far for a reason.* Use your knowledge and experience from the past wisely.

- No matter what you believe, what you have done, what you're willing to do, or where you're willing to go, there will always be somebody somewhere who will do all these things with you and somebody somewhere who won't. So don't allow yourself to be pushed into something that's just not "you." And please don't push others to do the same.

- As you are learning your way in this world, your friends and classmates are learning theirs. Learn from each other. Celebrate your differences. Treat each other fairly. You don't have to agree on everything, but *you don't have to hate, either.*

- I always say, "Oil and water don't mix, but you <u>can</u> hold them both in the same container." It's the same with this … maybe you won't "mix" with them or they with you, but it doesn't mean we can't all get along peacefully. Besides, you don't wanna lose focus of the real reason you came to college in the first place: to get an education!

3. **Clubs, Sports, and Academics** – As with a lot of the groups I've written about already, when it comes to acceptance and memberships, these groups aren't much different. They have expectations and responsibilities and are expected to perform and live up to a specific set of standards to accomplish them.

These clubs (including anything from fraternities and sororities to student government, marching bands and sports teams) will expect you to attend functions as well as participate in and endorse club or team events. The on-campus sports teams and marching bands will expect you to attend practices and games, work out, exercise, stay in shape, review game or practice footage, etc., and most will require you to hold a certain G.P.A. just to be able to qualify as a participating member.

The West Virginians

While I was attending Alderson-Broaddus University in Philippi, WV, (it was called "Alderson-Broaddus College" at the time) I was a member of "The West Virginians" (a premier touring ensemble of the music department that serves as ambassadors for Alderson-Broaddus University and for the state of West Virginia). This on-campus group had high expectations and demands of its members.

I remember we had to practice every Monday through Thursday from 4-6 p.m., take a 30-minute dinner break, and then resume practice until 8:30 p.m. (Did I mention this was *every* Monday through Thursday? Keep in mind I had class from 8 a.m.- 4 p.m. daily. Talk about not having much time to study!) On Fridays and weekends we traveled throughout the state and beyond, performing in high schools, churches and other venues, promoting our school, etc. This went on throughout the school year (we started our performances in August and would complete them in late June).

Not only were we expected to attend all practices and shows (which if you do the math is more than 200), we were also expected to memorize our lines and music, maintain a certain reputation that represented our school's beliefs and philosophies, attend chapel services twice a week AND keep a specific G.P.A.! All of this while staying fit, studying/doing homework, attending our daily classes *and* other on-campus functions! Whew! Talk about an eye-opener! I never had so much responsibility handed to me at one time up to this point in my life. It really was a challenge.

And this is nothing new. Colleges across the nation have been utilizing programs like this one and many others for years. It's not only a collegiate way of life, but in most schools, it's an expected way of life (and a good one, I might add). And that's just sports and the arts.

The academic societies on campus, although similar, may even be *more* strict. These groups often expect certain criteria to be met and upheld simply to have their name on your resume one day. You may even lose your title or position at your school if your academics don't meet very, *very* high academic and social expectations.

My Two Cents

- Regardless of which of these groups you participate in or patronize, please realize they were in existence long before you arrived on campus and they'll be there when you're gone. It's not their job to adapt to your ways or expectations.

- If you're going to succeed with any of these groups, you're going to have to see and do things *their* way. That doesn't mean that you can't encourage change or offer new ideas, it just means that for the most part these groups are already established and structured. (I had a real problem learning this and it cost me several friends and memories. I had such an attitude back then. It was *my way* or the highway. And guess who took the highway? Sigh.)

- *These groups don't need you as much as you need them.* So keep this in mind if you are considering being a part of any of these organizations during your college experience. If you're not prepared for what they want or expect, you may easily find yourself spending more time trying to become what they want or need than you are getting what you want and need ... which is an education!

4. **Traditions** – The fact that you're on campus is enough to allow you to become and feel a part of any school's traditions and its personality. College traditions are some of the best and most memorable traditions in existence. From week-long parties and ridiculous theatrics, to rites of passage and alumni events, these traditions are sometimes funded and attended by more students than many other major events on campus.

19

Depending upon their legality and pageantry, some will even garner national attention while others stay shrouded in secrecy.

"Take Me Home, Country Roads" And The Grove
Many traditions by colleges and universities are celebrated for the livelihood and sense of community that they bring to the campus. Traditions like *"Take Me Home, Country Roads"* at West Virginia University (where fans have been singing the famous hit song by John Denver at every home game since the early 70's) or *The Grove* at Ole Miss (where thousands gather at the legendary tailgating area located at the center of the campus to eat, celebrate, and of course, cheer their beloved "Hotty Toddy") are great examples of this. Both are longstanding traditions that are as much a part of the school as the people that attend them.

Other traditions are so well known and pique such interest that they draw thousands of people to the school annually, even when many of the people attending aren't affiliated with that school whatsoever.

Halloween At OU
I'm reminded of one such place: Ohio University. (Not to be confused with "The Ohio State University" in Columbus, Ohio, Ohio University, or "OU," is located within the surrounding hills of Athens, Ohio.)

Every year on or near Halloween, thousands and *thousands* of people from all over the state (and beyond) drive to OU (possibly to the school's dismay ... I honestly don't know) with their best or worst Halloween costume (depending upon your point of view) and parade up and down the street like it's a runway for models, combined with a little Vegas "Cirque du Soleil" and a dash of just about anything else you can think of (seriously). It is truly a sight to behold.

How do I know? I've been in attendance myself! Keep in mind, I've never had the privilege of being a student at OU. I was only there to visit some of my friends who were (and out of curiosity to see if all I had heard about this great school and tradition was true).

I'll never forget it. When I arrived on campus, I didn't have to walk far before I found a sea of people constantly moving up and down the streets of Athens in some of the craziest and funniest costumes I've ever seen in my life. Young or old. Elaborate or simple. Gorgeous or scary. It was quite a fascinating sight to behold and a great memory as well. One that I'll cherish forever. I had a lot of fun, met some great people, and managed to check out the campus all in one fun-filled weekend.

(I know, I know … You want some "juicy" details dontchya? Like what costume I wore or what I did that night, right? Well those details are for me to know and you to never find out! Ha! Besides, this book is about surviving college, not disclosing too much of my past party experiences. I will tell you this though, *I didn't do anything that night that I had to regret the next day*. I had a great time, yes, but I had a *safe* time, too. So keep that in mind the next time you go hopping around to different campus traditions.)

And just to be clear, I want you to know, I have nothing but the utmost respect for OU. Growing up in Little Hocking/Belpre, Ohio, I have several friends who attended OU, as well as former students who do now. They all have nothing but good things to say about this school (GO BOBCATS!) and I feel the same way. I simply wanted to use them and this school as an example of just how powerful a college tradition can be, with or without the school's backing.

What's The Point?
Why did I share that story? To make my point clear: college traditions are here and here to stay. And some are sooo strong and engraved within the fabric of the community (*sometimes regardless of the school's approval*) that they can pull an audience of people that don't even attend the very school from which the tradition was born. How sad would it be then, to be a student at your school and not see and celebrate such time-honored traditions your school offers while people who don't even attend your school do? It doesn't make any sense.

I'll elaborate more on this later, but just realize: the more involved you are with your school and what it celebrates, the less likely you are to drop out or transfer. In other words, you're more likely to survive your college experience (graduate). And that's the whole point of having this book, right?

Now … back to what I was saying …

Whatever the case may be, whether you attend traditional college festivities as a student or as a spectator, traditions are a very normal (and usually accepted) part of any college campus. If you're going to attend college, you're certainly going to become subjected to one or more of them during your stay.

21

My Two Cents

- Whatever your college's traditions may be, please know that you will most likely be expected to participate in one or more of them, and as long as they're legal, you probably should. They'll help you bond with your friends and your school and encourage a relationship that makes leaving school before your time less likely.

- Don't get involved in anything that goes against all you believe or stand for. (Sometimes a tradition can be legal but still considered unethical to individuals based upon foundational beliefs.)

- As long as what the group or activity is asking for is within reason, then by all means enjoy the festivities and the memories that come along with it. You don't wanna graduate only to find out that you missed out on something great and special that is respective to your school only (see chapter 27) or common within college life in general.

5. **Campus Personality (aka "Campus Culture")** – When it comes to campus personality, I'm not talking about a specific individual or group of individuals on campus. I'm actually talking about the personality that your campus has taken on due to the cultural atmosphere that resides there.

For example, some schools are located in remote areas and rural settings and have a very laid-back, Southern feel with a campus that's seemingly dominated by one or two ethnicities. Other schools may exist right in the heart of a major city or tourist area and have a very fast-paced urban vibe along with some of the most diverse groups of individuals in the world. Depending upon your campus setting, you may feel right at home and totally comfortable or you may feel quite misunderstood and totally out of place. This is what I mean when I refer to campus personality and how it can affect your time in college.

Knowing your college's campus personality is very important as it will help to explain why some things seem to "just work" for you while other things don't. If you're from a very rural town and your college's campus personality is very urban, you may find yourself having a hard time adjusting to the culture of your campus.

People may think you have an accent and "sound funny." Or maybe they think you look different and "dress funny." The same can be true if you're from the city and going to college in a rural area. This can be even more common if you're from another country. Although these possibilities do exist and can affect your level of comfort while at school, *they don't have to*.

The Giving Tree

When I was a young boy, my mother was in the backyard "operating" on a small tree. I saw her cutting limbs back and throwing manure on the base of the tree. I thought my mom was crazy! Why in the world would she take a perfectly good tree, cut its limbs, and then throw manure on it? It just didn't make any sense to me. So I decided to ask her.

She informed me that she was merely pruning the tree and that by doing so, it would grow back thicker and stronger next year. And as for the manure, she told me that it mixes with the ground to create some of the richest soil possible, allowing the tree to grow even healthier.

What? Are you serious? This was the craziest thing I'd ever heard!

And yet, it was true.

That tree grew back the following year taller, stronger and healthier than ever. To this day it is one of the biggest trees in my old neighborhood.

Who would've thought? Certainly not me. And you may think I was a little naïve and simple back then, but believe me, many of us are the same way today.

Sometimes people and life cut us back and then "throw manure all over us." This pruning can hurt at times and the stench of the manure can be overwhelming. However, we do have choices.

> **We can complain about the smell and the pain of what we feel, or we can use these experiences to grow, and grow stronger.**

Remember, a college's campus personality is just that … it's the college's personality, *not yours*. It doesn't have to be "the Great Melting Pot" that all students are poured into, melting into one. It's just the personality of the campus overall. Your presence there doesn't have to collide with it or confront it. On the contrary, it can *add* to it. Think of it more like a salad bowl and less like a melting pot and I think you'll get the idea. The more you add to the salad, the more flavor it has.

Your presence on campus can be the same way. So don't let the fact that you don't "look green and leafy like all the other lettuce" knock you outta school. Oftentimes, students will mistake their lack of comfort on campus (due to its personality) for a feeling of "This place just isn't for me. No one 'gets' me here. I think I may have chosen the wrong school." I've seen this happen far too often and most of the time the end result isn't good. Rather than the individual student celebrating their differences and sharing them with others, the student usually ends up transferring to another school or worse yet, dropping out. It shouldn't be this way, and it doesn't have to be.

My Two Cents

- Not "perfectly" fitting in is *great*. It allows you to shine where others simply fade. Sure all those opinions about your accent, the way you dress, or what you believe in can be harsh, but life is not about what happens to you, but rather, how you respond to it.

- When people on campus make fun of how you talk or dress or what you believe, I want you to know that as harsh as all of these opinions may sound, that's all they are … opinions.

- Even if what everyone is saying about you is actually true, who cares? It doesn't mean you need to transfer or drop outta school! It just means you're different (which I think is cool anyway). I've heard it said many times before and I'll state it myself, **"You were born an original, so don't live as someone else's clone."**

- Being a little different is not only okay, it's *preferred*. It will show others your originality and allow you to show value in areas where others can't.

My Solution

As with any group, what makes it an actual "group" are the things that differentiate it from others. If these groups didn't have some sort of guidelines, rules, or belief system then they wouldn't be a "group" and if that were the case, what would be the point in joining them?

Being a part of something that is different and exclusive can be very rewarding and create a sense of belonging. I certainly encourage you to be a part of anything in college that has a positive impact on your time while you're there. It will increase the odds of you staying in school, staying in *that* particular school, and graduating on time. However, **don't let any group pressure you or force you to say or do anything that makes you truly uncomfortable**.

Know Thyself

There's a difference between not *wanting* to do something and knowing you *shouldn't* do something. Please know the difference and do what's best for you. If you have any doubts or questions, ask someone you know, trust and love for advice (preferably someone older with experience who has "been there, done that"). They will be able to help you decide whether you should just grow-up and do it or simply say no and walk away.

Please know, however, that if you decide *not* to participate in or join a particular group, it doesn't mean you still can't go to that school and get your education. Don't let a membership in one group or a lack of one in another cause you to drop out of school. Besides, most likely there is another group right across campus that would love to take you just as you are.

So enjoy your college experience and live free! Life is too short for unnecessary pressure and stress.

Chapter 2

College Life – The Pressure To Fit In

This section is an extension of what I've mentioned previously concerning "The Five Common Senses" and the pressures that college students often face while starting or continuing their college career. However, as the previous guidelines dealt with many of the pressures coming from a college's groups, organizations, or campus culture, this section will deal more with the pressure that may come from the media, friends or your own self-doubt.

You are getting older. What worked for you in high school may or may not work for you now. There are new opportunities (good and bad) offered to you now on a daily basis that may not have existed in your world a few years ago (or even a few months ago, for that matter). Everything you've learned up to this point can and oftentimes will be challenged. This can be a good thing as it causes you to solidify your reasoning for your foundational beliefs and build upon them. But it can be scary, too.

What if the opposing views sound credible? What if they're convincing?

What if they're right?

Having a new understanding or viewpoint on a particular topic or ideal can be a very healthy thing. It's an indication that you are growing and broadening the "library" that exists within your mind. But please know, you didn't learn all that you know up to this point overnight, or even in a month or two, so please don't feel you have to change it all overnight or in a month or two, either.

Truth is one thing, perception is another. If you've ever heard me speak at a conference, you may have heard me mention the fact that the word "lie" is right smack dab in the middle of the word "believe." Isn't that somethin'? Ironically, there is some truth to that.

> ### *What we often believe to be true or false is heavily determined by our own perception.*

I've always told people, "The interpretation of art tells us more about the interpreter than it does about the art being interpreted." This is very similar to that concept. When it comes to the world around us, what's popular, necessary, desirable or even attainable in the "actual world" can be drastically different from that which is attainable in our "perceived world."

If you watch the latest movies, TV shows, news broadcasts, commercials, etc., then you are bombarded on a daily basis with what you *should* be wearing, eating, doing, being, buying, and more.

Michael Jackson's Red Jacket

It reminds me of a documentary I was watching the other day about Michael Jackson and his life. During part of the show, they played live footage from 1983/84 showcasing several of his fans from around the world. During this time, Michael's album, *Thriller*, was breaking all kinds of sales records around the world. Two videos in particular, "Thriller" and "Beat It," had become very popular and were being played seemingly everywhere. In both videos, Michael is seen wearing a red (leather?) jacket. Although both jackets are different, they're very similar and very prominent in the videos.

Now … Let me ask you … What do you think about a zillion of those fans I saw in that documentary were wearing? You guessed it! Red leather jackets! Was this a bad thing? No, not necessarily. They liked Michael, they liked his jacket. No big deal. But the power that such advertising possesses (directly or indirectly) can be dangerous if not harnessed correctly.

It's one thing to emulate your favorite rockstar's clothing or personal style, it's another to let it consume you to the point that you no longer have your own.

So be careful. Advertisers and big businesses understand this power very well. In fact, they're counting on it to work its magic on you, in hopes of making them a profit with whatever it is they're selling. Many of them will weave together some of the catchiest songs with the coolest videos, as well as the hottest places and some the sexiest people they can find on this planet into the trendiest TV shows, magazines, or movies you've ever seen.

And why? They do it all in hopes that you will want what they have and actually believe you are incomplete without it (clothing, style, jewelry, music, etc.). If you're not careful, you may perceive and actually believe the lie they are telling you. The lie that says you are missing out on sooo much fun, excitement, sexiness and popularity if you don't have their product. It can be very detrimental to who you are, what you believe, and your success in college.

> *I know people who felt totally comfortable and perfectly fine with who they were and what they believed __UNTIL__ they went to college!*

Their *actual world* was great, but the way they were told to perceive their world was another. Whether it be due to local advertising, the campus's culture and personality, or simply due to now being a resident in a different region on this planet (city, state or country), once they arrived on campus they soon fell prey to the belief that they were out of style, out of touch, and far behind those around them living at the same level.

Mary, Mary ... Why You Buggin'?

It was the summer before my freshman year of college. I was at a party with some friends of mine when I met Mary. She had the most beautiful green eyes and the richest Southern accent I'd ever heard. She was very much a "plain Jane" (and this was a good thing) and *very* courteous (those Southern girls never lack hospitality!) She was the kind of girl you marry and take home to mom if you know what I mean.

At least at that moment she was ...

Mary soon left for college (I'll keep the school anonymous, but I will tell you her new school was about four hours north of her hometown) and she wasn't on the campus more than a week or two before she came to the (unfortunate) belief that her clothes were wrong, her speech was wrong, and her look, style and personality were all wrong. She immediately began to take drastic measures to change *all* of it and fit in with everyone and everything. Spending money on things she couldn't afford (all those college student credit card offers ... Ugh! more on those later), paying for food, clothing, party favors, etc. that she didn't need, trying to be something she wasn't (from her clothing and music to her beliefs and speech) and losing herself in the process.

What a horrible, horrible thing to do!

28

Mary's new ways and lifestyle had a detrimental effect, not only on her college experience, but her personal character as well. She started hanging out with the wrong people (you know the type ... the kind that skip class, party all the time, and think college is just an extension of high school with fewer rules). Although she did manage to make it through her freshman year (barely), she unfortunately dropped out of college during her sophomore year due to poor grades and becoming pregnant.

Talk about believing the hype. She, unfortunately, became the perfect example.

Listen to me. **You don't have to fit into someone else's world in order to belong in yours!** What got you this far in life got you this far for a reason.

Don't be like Mary ... DON'T BE**LIE**VE THE HYPE!

You don't need everything these media types or "friends" try to sell you. YOU are FAR BETTER than that! Believe me. And if you ever doubt my words, just remember, you didn't go to college to get a lifestyle makeover, you went to get an education! So do that instead.

Mirror, Mirror On The Wall ...
Based upon what I've stated previously, I want you to know that I am not saying you cannot change your style or look or personality. And I'm not saying your ideologies and viewpoints don't need improvement, either. Maybe they do? And maybe you DO need to change some things about your style. That's actually the beauty of a great college education and many of the great college professors that come with it: they both will spar with you and challenge much of what you know and believe. (And this is a good thing, believe me. It will build your character and enhance your personality.) Changing *some* of your ways when you get to college can be very practical and necessary. But changing *all* of them can be hazardous to your survival.

My Solution

As I've stated before, one of the great things about college (especially if you attend one that's a good distance from home) is that you can somewhat start your life all over again if you want ... new friends, new organizations, new town, new reputation, clean slate. That can be a rare and beautiful opportunity in itself. I just want you to know that although you can, *you don't have to.*

Do You See What I See?
Please realize there's a difference between *wanting* to do something and *needing* to do something. Don't let your perception of your actual world become clouded

with lies from an unrealistic, imposed world. And you definitely don't wanna allow it to cause you to leave school.

You are a rare and beautiful gift. There is not one other person exactly like you on this planet. Like I said before, why on Earth would you ever want to become someone else's clone? Live *free.* How you perceive the world and how I perceive it will be inherently different by nature. Enjoy your world. Decorate your world. *Live* in your world. Change it as much as you want as often as you want, but *only if* you want. What you need and what you're told you need are two different things.

The TRUTH is, the bill is yours, the debt is yours, and the consequences are yours, so why not let the decisions be yours? (Yeah … read that one again.)

Chapter 3
Are You Homesick or Lovesick?

I know you probably think you're sooo beyond being homesick and maybe you believe feeling lovesick could never apply to you. But don't be too quick to dismiss such "illnesses." I've seen many, many students do poorly in college (and some even transfer or drop out!) due to these illnesses that they swore would never get to them.

Taking One For The Team
Now granted, students will never admit that these illnesses were the source or the cause of why they drop out or transfer. Typically, students who suffer from these illnesses tend to blame their departure on other reasons that sound much more admirable. Reasons such as "My family is going through a tough time right now and they really need me back home" or "My church has a major situation that needs my help and if I don't help them, who will?"

Although these causes may be great and noble reasons to leave school now, please realize that staying in school and graduating will help you help them even that much more (more knowledge and more experience, not to mention your degree and all the financial possibilities that come with it). Besides that, of all the times I've known any student to leave school for family or church (or other such reasons), I've never known any of these reasons to be the *main* reason these students left. Not even once!

As a matter of fact, the students I've known to leave school for such reasons always had an ulterior reason for going home. Wanna take a guess at what it was? Their ulterior reason (or as I like to say, "The *real* reason") for leaving college and going back home always came down to one of two things:

31

- **They missed their family, friends and home life.**
- **They missed their girlfriend or boyfriend back home.**

Now I'm sure somebody somewhere has left college for reasons other than those two. Reasons like failing grades, lack of money, poor health, death in their immediate family, unplanned pregnancies, military obligations, and more. Although these may be necessary (and sometimes good) reasons to leave school, these are reasons that are "cause and effect." In other words, because one thing happened, the other *had* to happen.

In scenarios such as these, you basically "do what ya gotta do." But these aren't the reasons I'm referring to. I'm talking about reasons that aren't created due to the "cause and effect" syndrome. The two reasons I've listed above are due to unforeseen "illnesses" that, in their worst form, ail you until you give in to the pressure and transfer or drop out of school altogether. Believe me. It happens. I know for a fact. Why?

Because it happened to me.

And So It Goes ...
I'll never forget it ... it was October of my freshman year at Alderson-Broaddus University. The leaves were falling, there was a slight chill in the air, and it was a "lazy Sunday" to say the least. It was by all accounts, the perfect day for a walk, a game of touch football, or even a "Sunday drive."

So what was I doing? Where was I on this glorious day? Was I out enjoying the October air? Taking a stroll across campus with my new friends or playin' touch football on the campus with my suite mates? No ... not me. Not "Mr. I don't need anybody or anything 'cause I'm too cool." (I had *such* an attitude back then ... it was bad.)

Where was I? Believe it or not, I was locked away in my dorm room, lying on the floor in the fetal position, bawling my eyes out incessantly while I listened to the same song over and over ("And So It Goes" by Billy Joel, in case you're wondering). I was sick. Yes. I was sick. I had a case of lovesickness combined with a slight dose of homesickness.

And to make matters worse, *I didn't even know there was a cure.*

As I lay on the floor crying, I rehearsed over and over all the memories of my ex-girlfriend back home who had recently parted ways with me, as well as what I coulda, shoulda and woulda done differently if I only had one more chance with her. Reliving those memories only made me miss her and everything else that went with her (my home, my parents, my friends) that much more.

Yes, I was a mess. And every minute, every hour, every thought, and every tear I was spending to pay for the ability to rehearse such memories coulda and shoulda been spent on the current things in my life that deserved just as much honor and attention. Things like my grades, projects, book reports, new friends, studying, or even fun! (Imagine that.)

I Like To Move It, Move It

Although these things deserved just as much attention as my past (and in my opinion now, even more), they were being robbed of their rightful place in my life now because of something from back then.

Now don't get me wrong …

> **I do believe it's okay to miss home. I also believe it's okay to miss someone from your past. And honestly, I even believe it's okay to cry and feel lost at some point.**

Everybody does. *It's natural.*

But please know, you don't have to stay in this state of mind, reliving these feelings over and over again. Give honor where honor is due, yes, but then <u>be done with it</u>. If you need to take a day or two to deal with missing your home, your friends, your family, or your loved ones, then so be it. Do whatever you gotta do to get it outta your system. But after that, you gotta move on.

(Notice I didn't say you gotta get rid of them. I just said you gotta move on).

Some people are meant to stay in your heart forever, but only in your life for a season. Others will be in your heart and your life forever, which means they'll be there for you when you go home for the holiday break, weekend visits, and next summer's vacation. So don't be offended when I say you gotta move on. I just mean for now.

The sooner you can realize this, the better and easier your life will be. The people who will be in your heart and life forever – people like your friends (some of them) or family back home – perhaps you're just missing them because you haven't seen them in a while. It's not like you're never gonna see these people again. Most likely they'll still be right where you left them when you go back home, and when you do you can catch up with them all you want. But please know, just as you were excited to be going off to college, they were excited for you as well (and still are). And although I'm sure they miss you, too, in the long run they'll be so glad you stayed in school and finished (especially those that wish they had the opportunity that you have now). Besides, four years is nothin'! It'll be done before you know it (look how fast high school went by). So keep it movin'.

There's a whole world out there waiting for you to introduce yourself to it and it needs you and everything you have to offer.

So don't make it wait longer than it should for you to graduate and bring to it all the new knowledge and experience you will soon own that comes with your degree. Don't sit out a semester (which adds time to your graduation date) or drop out altogether just because you're homesick or lovesick or feeling overwhelmed.

Stay in school. Focus on your work. Graduate on time.

You CAN do it. *Believe me.*

No Pain, No Gain?

I'll never forget it. It was a hot day in the middle of July and I had until October 3rd to get myself in shape. I was tired of feeling sluggish, tired of feeling out of shape, and tired of feeling tired. I had recently signed up for Morgan's Little Miami Triathlon (near Cincinnati, Ohio) where my buddy, Fred Reeder (editor of this book), and I would be expected, as a team, to canoe 6 miles, jog 5.5 miles, and then bike 18 miles. Our goal at this point was simple: Finish the race, and don't finish last.

As I began training for the event, I quickly realized how out of shape I truly was and that getting to a place where completing this triathlon was even possible may be a bigger task than I had originally thought. The exercises and reps I was attempting were very difficult and hard to complete.

I remember looking at my personal trainer, Reggie, and saying, "I don't think I can do this. This is harder than what I thought." At that point, Reggie looked at me, and although what he said was very simple and succinct, it has resonated in my ears for years:

"It may seem hard now … but if it were easy *everybody* would do it. You're here for a reason, and it's not so you can quit and go back home."

Reggie wasn't talking about college, obviously, but his advice concerning my workout works for you and your college experience, as well. You didn't come this far to turn back now. If it *were* easy perhaps everybody *would* do it. Research shows only about 27-29% of Americans have a college degree. That's about 3 out of every 10 people. (Or think of it this way: 7 out of every 10 people *don't* have a degree!) If that's the case, then *you are rare*. And you've been given a rare opportunity. So don't turn back now.

Reggie was right ... You ARE here for a reason, and it's not so you can quit and go back home.

Believe me. If anybody has ever suffered in college due to homesickness, lovesickness, a feeling of inadequacy, or even fear, *I have*. I had started college only to quit. (I forfeited the remainder of my scholarship, and dropped out.) I allowed these feelings (and many others) to defeat me for two years before I finally went back, finished my schooling, and earned my degree. Taking those two years off wasn't worth it, either. I wish I would've stayed in school and finished the first time around.

So learn from my mistakes, please. If you're going to make mistakes, that's fine, but just make sure they're new ones and not the ones I've already warned you about. Life (and school) has enough tests for you already. No need to keep taking the same ones over and over, right? Besides, if I did it without this book and the advice in it, surely you can do it with it. ☺

Oh ... and by the way ... my buddy and I <u>did</u> finish the triathlon, and we <u>didn't</u> finish last! (If I could put a sound bite in here right now it would say something like, "Oooohh ... What's my name? Who's the man?! Whoooo!" But since I can't, you'll just have to imagine what I would sound like saying it! ☺ Hey, a guy can brag, can't he? *You* try completing a triathlon! It's work!)

My Solution

When it comes to being homesick or lovesick, there are ways to prevent such illnesses from ever occurring. Much like a good dose of Vitamin C on a daily basis will help boost your immune system and prevent sickness, so too will a daily dose of the right thoughts and a correct game plan help boost your confidence and prevent the occurrence of sickness in love or of home.

I Love It When A Plan Comes Together
What I suggest is that you get a plan. If you are a "Mama's boy" or a "Daddy's girl" (and there's nothing wrong with that!) then you may want to set at time each week to contact your parents and get your "fix." And with today's

technological advancements, this is easier than ever (phone call, text message, webcam, email, video conferencing, social networks, etc.). Hearing their voice and getting their advice or seeing their faces and catching their smiles can be very soothing and quite useful, especially during your early stages of college.

I will warn you, though … I do not suggest that you call or contact them every single day (or anyone else back home for that matter). At some point, you have to begin to take on the new life and maturity level that you will be held accountable for. But for now, if contacting them every Tuesday and Thursday night for an hour conversation is what it's going to take for you to get things going until you feel more comfortable in your "new world" then go for it! Whatever you can do to increase and improve your odds of staying in school is a plus.

Home, Sweet Home!

Another thing you can do to prevent such illnesses is to simply go home and visit occasionally. This can help give you that quick fix that you so desperately crave after only a week or two out on your own. However, as I stated previously with the contact, I do NOT recommend that you do this more than necessary. Going home *every* weekend is a bad idea (see "The Other '75/25 Rule'" in Chapter 23). It will only slow down your progress of building and living successfully in your new world. A healthy diet of home visitation (for any student living two hours or less away from home) consists of a home visit once every four or five weeks. In the meantime, just call home or stay in contact through various types of communication.

You can also put up a few pictures of your friends and family in your room or perhaps a favorite item or prop from home that helps bring a small part of your home-life to your new life. This can help to give you a "home away from home" feeling while staying on campus. As with everything else we've discussed, there are limits to these as well (see Chapter 24 for my advice and warnings concerning dorm room decorations).

She Loves Me, She Loves Me Not

When it comes to being lovesick, if you are dealing with anything like I was during my freshman year, the best thing you can do is let her (or him) go. Don't get caught up in what you should've done. Instead, get focused on what you need to be doing – Studying!

If they're an "ex" just remember this:

Ex-girlfriends and ex-boyfriends are exes for a reason.

And if they're *not* your ex and you are still dating (and you simply miss them like crazy), you may want to ask yourself these questions:

- Why am I dating someone so seriously at such a young age?
- Is this really a perfect dating/relationship scenario?
- If we're perfect for each other, why is he/she somewhere else while I'm here?

These are some serious questions to consider. I mean, think of it this way: if you had a son or daughter, would you want them dating someone in another school or even another state while spending thousands of dollars attempting to get them an education and graduate? Especially in their early twenties?

Listen … you have enough on your plate already. The last thing you need is drama added to it. If you wanna stay in a long-distance relationship, you can. That's your prerogative. But know this, *the longer you are here and they are there, the more likely it is that you will begin to grow apart from each other.* Eventually you're gonna want someone to go to the game with, someone to sit with at the movies, someone to make new memories with. You've moved on to a new school and new town, and new ways. Perhaps it's time to move on in your love life, too? (Just a suggestion … Don't be mad at me here … I'm on *your* side, remember?)

Besides, if you feel you MUST date someone during your college years, why not date someone on campus? At least they'll be able to share in your good and bad times, as well as having several of the same friends, professors and memories. If you're gonna have a "tag-team partner," at least get one who's in the same ring with ya. I'm just sayin'.

Chapter 4
What To Do When Nobody Knows Who You Are

Well I hate to be the bearer of bad news, but unless the college you are attending is expecting your arrival with great anticipation for some great talent or skill you bring to its institution, then the odds are, you'll be just another name and number … a "nobody." And please don't take offense to that.

When I say "nobody" I don't mean that you're no longer important or special or that you simply don't matter. All I'm saying is, compared to how you've been living, going from where you were to where you are (or will be) will certainly make you feel like you're no longer important or special (to some degree). But don't lose hope! Things *can* get better. However, it will take a little patience and work on your part to see it through.

Let me give you an example …

The Price Of Fame
Let's say you attended an average high school in a typical suburban school district. While in this school, you managed to rack up a few high school records. You know … perhaps you were the track star, or the head cheerleader. Maybe you could throw a fastball like nobody else, or spike a volleyball harder than anyone in the state. Maybe your name is hanging on a banner in your high school gymnasium, or perhaps you were in the honors program and held every form of student office and position available from Class President to Valedictorian.

Whatever the case may be, when you were in high school, you were "it." Everybody in your school, from the incoming freshman to the principal and superintendent, knew your name. You could go to the local mall and practically feel like a celebrity.

If any of these possibilities fit your high school life and times, then you are well-accustomed to recognition, acceptance and notoriety. Do this for four years and you may actually begin to believe this is the way life works. (It's not, by the way.) Then you wake up one day and you find yourself on a college campus that has more students than your hometown has residents! Or in a classroom that has more desks than your church has members!

Talk about an eye-opener!

> **You now find you can walk across campus all day,
> _any_ day and not even ONE person knows your name,
> let alone your prior accomplishments!**

What? Nobody???

Yes! NOBODY. Not even ONE.

You realize in just a short amount of time, that you've gone from being a "somebody" back home to becoming a "nobody" on campus. And I'm willing to bet you don't like it, either. (I know I didn't!)

My Solution

The solution for this problem requires two things: _patience_ and _understanding._

As time goes on, you will automatically get to know people and they will get to know you. It's inevitable. You'll begin to learn your professors, your suite mates, your sorority sisters, your fraternity brothers, your band mates, your classmates, etc. The list goes on and on. It's just a matter of time.

I Am Legend
Whatever you did back home that impressed your friends and family still holds true to this point. So most likely it will become known, at least to some degree, to your new friends and mates within your "new world" now. Eventually they'll see or hear about how well you can throw that ball, jump that hurdle, give that speech, or sing that song. So be patient. If you're not the "Big man on campus" yet (or woman, for that matter), it doesn't mean you can't be eventually.

If you *are* fortunate to become "it" again on your new college campus (notice I said "if"), it <u>will</u> take a little time. So relax. You didn't earn that respect over night back home and you won't do it here either. (This is where patience comes in.) In the meantime, don't confuse the lack of popularity and notoriety for a belief that "Nobody 'gets' me here" or "I chose the wrong school. Back home people love me. But here, nobody cares." Those statements simply aren't true.

Nobody caring and nobody knowing aren't the same things.

Once you understand and realize this, you will be more likely to accept everyone's lack of interest in who you are at the moment and focus on why you actually came to college (to get an education).

Now for the understanding ...

The "It" Factor
What you need to understand is the fact that it is actually possible that you do <u>not</u> become "it" on your new college campus. *And that's okay.*

Success in college is not synonymous with whether everybody knows your name before you leave it.

I can think of many, *many* college star athletes who seemingly everybody knew while they were on campus who never finished their degree. (I could easily name five right now right off the top of my head, but I don't want to bring anymore unnecessary negative attention to their school simply because these people failed to "do the right thing.") Many of these stars, whether they flunked out (too much partying, poor grades, skipping classes) or were kicked out (breaking NCAA rules, getting arrested, challenging school authority, etc.), did NOT finish college and graduate, although they were (and many still are) VERY well known. (Some have even graced the cover of popular magazines and made headlines around the nation for their athletic skill and expertise, only to find themselves locked in prison only two or three years later, now *without* a degree, and *with* a permanent record!)

HOWEVER ... I also know of *several* college students who left college as quietly as they entered it, yet graduated and went on to succeed in their careers and lives. Who are they? They're the everyday people all around you! They're teachers, lawyers, professors, doctors, business owners, etc. You probably know many of them already and don't even realize it. And why don't you realize it? Because they did exactly what I'm telling you to do: They focused on their degree and graduating on time, and NOT on trying to be "all that," attempting to make their college experience as popular as their high school days.

40

Everybody Knows My Name (Kind Of ...)

One of my former students (we'll call her "Deanna") was very popular while in high school. (I had the privilege of teaching her during her junior year.) She played on the girls' varsity basketball team and was very active in our school's programs, too. By her senior year, practically everyone in our school knew Deanna. You didn't even have to say her full name. Just say "Deanna" and teachers, students and parents (even the superintendent) knew exactly who you were talking about. To say that she was popular in our school would be an understatement.

To make a long story short, Deanna graduated from our school with flying colors and received a full scholarship (playing basketball) to a nearby university in the state of Kentucky. While there, she managed to successfully represent her school, not only through basketball, but also by participating in several on-campus activities and events (which was very smart by the way). She completed her degree in only four years and now has a successful career in business.

Ironically, unlike her high school days, if you go to the university she attended and ask students or staff if they know her or remember her, some people will, *some people won't.*

Why? Because **her goal wasn't to be the biggest, baddest, coolest, smartest, prettiest, richest, most popular girl at her school** (to be honest, it never was in high school, either). She simply went to college to get her degree and pursue her career (and she did just that). Anything else was just a bonus.

Did she make her mark while she was there? Of course! She did exactly as she had in high school, participating in campus activities, playing ball, helping her community, etc. But she didn't lose sight of why she was *really* there (to get her degree), and she didn't let the fact that she was no longer the "Big Man on Campus" (or woman, in this case) distract her from getting it.

Listen to me ...

When it comes to your college career, popularity does not equal success ... Graduation does.

Deanna entered and exited college *quietly.*

She never played basketball on national television.

She never made the cover of a sports magazine.

She never broke any NCAA records or obtained any championship titles.

She never signed a big contract with the WNBA to play professional ball.

So was she successful?

ABSOLUTELY.

Why?

Because it's not about what she didn't do, but rather, what she did do.

She did go to college.

She did pick a school that was giving her a scholarship for her athletic ability (no student loans! Yesssssss!)

She did graduate and get her degree! (She *survived* college.)

She did graduate on time (she completed a four-year program in exactly four years … imagine that!)

And FYI- **Deanna was raised by her mother in a single-parent home, as a minority, with no brothers or sisters!**

> *If you're not immediately recognized when you arrive on campus, or even if you're not four years later, it doesn't mean you weren't successful. It might just mean you were* **focused***.*

So don't sweat it. Focus on your grades, make the most of your opportunities to meet new friends, professors and classmates, and take advantage of opportunities that can promote you in a positive way. These things can and will make your college experience more enjoyable. They will increase your odds of becoming "it" again (at least to some degree) while increasing your odds of staying in your school (and graduating from it).

Chapter 5
How To Deal with Test Stress

Your first exams at college are often real eye-openers. Not necessarily because they're so difficult, but because they're so different. You will be surprised at just how much will be expected of you from one professor (wait until you read Chapter 16) and how little will be expected from you by another.

One professor may expect you to read 80-100 pages within two days and then give you a quiz over what you read, while another professor may never require any written work until taking the mid-term and simply want to discuss the text with you during class. Some classes will demand a ton of your time, energy and research skill, while other classes will be so simple they're practically a party.

(Hey, I actually took a bowling class in college! Talk about fun!) Whatever the case or class may be, stress doesn't have to be a part of it.

Stress = Mess
Research indicates that stress can have a very powerful, negative effect on the human body. It can keep you up all night, rob you of your sleep, mess with your eating habits, and in some cases, even affect your short-term memory. This type of stress tends to come by way of being unprepared, not having a plan, poor study habits, or simply the fear of something new. (Maybe you've thought or said something like, "I've never had a teacher like this before... This lady is impossible!" or "I'll never pass *his* class! I *hate* this subject.")

During your first few months of school, the stress can be overwhelming (if you let it). But it doesn't have to be. With the proper plan and a little understanding, you can virtually eliminate any test stress you may have. Don't let it get you down. If you do, it will. And if it does, your grades will follow suit. And then you wake up one day near the end of the semester questioning everything that got you here in the first place.

Questions like:
- Am I smart enough for college?
- Is this really the place for me?
- Am I *really* ready for this?
- Should I just wait and come back next year?

As I informed so many students before, allow me to inform you as well: Don't believe the hype! You're *fine*. These questions and feelings are normal.

You *can* do it and I *will* help. (Smile.)

My Solution

When it comes to dealing with test stress, there are several keys available to help you eliminate it altogether (or at least reduce a lot of it). One key is to simply have a plan. Another is to form an alliance. (Both of these keys are dealt with in a much more specific manner in Chapters 14 and 16.) Other ways include something as simple as eating healthier foods (fruits and vegetables) and/or exercising three or more times per week. I could go on and on, but rather than going into a dissertation about how to deal with this stress, let me just say what I've stated before and will again and again: If you heed my warnings, accept my challenges, and adhere to my advice, your college experience will not only be successful, but a lot of fun as well (and stress-free!) Your solution to this problem is this book itself! Read it. All of it! Make notes in the text, highlight your favorite parts, and then reread it again (at least the parts you need most) throughout your college journey.

Remember, I've been where you are. I've felt your fear and stress.

And look where I am now.

Believe me …You <u>CAN</u> do this and I <u>WILL</u> help, but you can't quit. I know it's tough. I know you feel alone. I know you're doubtful. Those feelings are all normal. Seriously. But you can't let them keep you from your dream. You made it this far for a reason, so don't quit on me now.

You hear me?

DON'T QUIT!

Chapter 6

Everyday Problems All College Students Face

There's nothing worse than being miles away from home, on your own, and finding yourself having to deal with things that, in the past, were never an issue. Things like being very sick and in need of something as simple as a warm bowl of your mother's soup and loving touch. Or how about wishing you had your dad there on campus with his mechanical expertise and golden touch when your car starts making "that noise." Perhaps you just wish you had someone to work out with at the gym like you did back home, or someone to help with the little things that make life *"life."* Well college is no different.

When you're away from home, then you are *away* from home. All the problems that come with it (life) will follow you to school, and if you're not careful you may find yourself having a bit of a hard time with what used to be fairly simple tasks. Things like getting your laundry done, finding a ride to the store, having someone to talk to, or even dealing with being sick.

As trivial as these things may sound, you'd be surprised how many students aren't prepared to deal with one or more of them.

Springsteen
So it's the middle of my freshman year, sometime in January, and I'm sick as can be. Although I didn't know exactly what it was at the time, I later found that I had come down with a serious case of the flu.

Now being sick is one thing, but being sick two hours away from home, with no medicine, no money, and no mom is even worse. I felt horrible. It *was* horrible.

45

I remember lying there on my bed in my dorm room, alone, waiting for my father to come get me. (I had made the phone call home and asked that someone puh-leez come pick me up!) Due to the length of the drive and his work schedule, my dad didn't arrive until almost 11 p.m. that night (I had phoned home around 3 p.m.). While I waited for his arrival, I cried. (Yes, I know, I know … I'm supposed to be a "man" and be tough, but I was a mama's boy and I was in pain. Real pain. Physical pain. So … I cried.)

The longer I lay there, the more I began to question what I was doing there to begin with. I mean, why did I choose this college? Did I really need to be this far away from home? Where are all my friends? Other than the help of Christina (see my original group of Super Friends in chapter 9) I felt very alone.

As the minutes turned into hours, the questions continued … Does anybody even understand how I feel? What in the world am I doing here? I don't even really like it here. What's the point?

The longer I waited, the more I hated.

I was in physical pain, yes, but I began to stack reason upon reason of why I should just leave this school and go back home. And why? Because the school was sooo bad? Because my new friends weren't real friends? Because this place really just wasn't for me? No … those weren't the reasons at all. They had nothing to do with why I felt the way I did.

> ## The truth of the matter is, for the first time in my life, I was sick <u>and</u> alone … at the same time.

Miserable? Yes.

But needing to drop out and move back home? Uh … NO!

Wanting my family, wanting to be home in my old bed, wanting to feel my mother's touch with a warm bowl of soup and a soothing word … those are all reasonable things to want and desire (and there's nothing wrong with doing so). But I also needed to snap out of it and see the situation for what it was.

My new school or new friends … They had nothing to do with my sickness or how I felt. I was simply sick. Nothing more, nothing less. Just physically sick.

It reminds me of an old Bruce Springsteen song that contains the following lyrics:

"Everybody needs a place to rest, everybody wants to have a home. Don't make no difference what nobody says. Ain't nobody like to be alone."

I couldn't have said it better myself.

As I've stated before in many ways and will again and again, don't confuse the issue. I didn't need a new school or new friends. I didn't need to drop out of my current school and move back home. I just needed to not be sick. That's all. Plain and simple.

Believe it or not, many students end up confusing the loss of help with issues like this one and many other simple life tasks with that common feeling of "This place just isn't for me. Nobody 'gets me' here. I think I'm going to transfer to a school back home or possibly even drop out."

Rather than making their grades and leaving school with their degree, they simply *make their exit and leave their school.* It's sad, but it happens. Fortunately for you, it doesn't have to. ☺

My Solution

If you truly want to survive your college experience successfully then you've got to find some friends. You know, friends that can help you when you're in a tough situation, or in this case, when you're sick. But these won't be just any friends. These friends will be your "Super Friends."

And why do I call them Super Friends and not just "friends?" Because just as a superhero has a specific ability or power that helps him or her help those around them, you need to pick very specific friends for their individual ability or "power" to help you and then befriend them. And all of these Super Friends don't need to be your closest friends or members of your sorority or fraternity, etc. Some can be acquaintances if necessary.

The point is, you need to pick your Super Friends and pick them according to the power they possess in regard to the need that you have. They will play a major role in your overall collegiate success. However, their role in your life will deal more with the typical day-to-day activities and necessary tasks that life requires of you and not with your grades or academic studies (we'll save that for the alliance you'll be forming after you read Chapter 16).

The beautiful (and yet strange) thing about this group is that *they don't even need to know they're a member of your Super Friends group in order for them*

47

to fulfill their role successfully. If you choose them wisely, all they'll have to do is be themselves in order for you to benefit from their "super power."

Now am I suggesting that you try to deceive these people and use them without their knowledge of it?

Of course not!

It's just that having them in your life (or at least in your "college life") is good enough for you to accomplish your goals with their help. If you want (or prefer) to include them in on what you're doing (and I certainly think that is fine if you do), then by all means go for it! As a matter of fact, get 'em a copy of this book and let them share in your plan. *It would actually make your chances of success even greater.*

Many of the problems you will face during your college experience can be solved simply by having the right people around you at the right time.

We Interrupt This Program ...

To drive home the concept and the necessity of having your own group of Super Friends, I have decided to list two specific problems (transportation and money) that many students face during their college career and explain how *I* solved these problems for myself (with the help of my Super Friends) to give you a better understanding of exactly how to do it and just how easy it is.

Although transportation and money may not be issues for you, please read these next two chapters in their entirety, as the strategy to go about obtaining both will be a useful template for you to use in the pursuit of other necessary items and solutions for many of the problems that you will face during your college experience.

I also give you my suggestions concerning work, should you decide to get a job while in school, and how to do it with the least amount of stress on your chances of survival.

So take good notes! These stories aren't just "stories," they're solutions for problems that will knock you out of your chances of surviving college if you're not careful.

Chapter 7

So You Think You Need a Car?

ATTENTION! I realize that several of you reading this do not need a car. For you, transportation is not an issue. However, as mentioned previously, please understand the car in the problem I've listed next is simply a symbol of any tangible thing you may need but unfortunately are missing during your college experience.

And while I'm at it, please realize, it's not so much about what you need, but rather, *it's about what you need to do to get what you need.* For me, it was a car. For you, perhaps something totally different. Either way, I believe the solution for this problem will be of great use to you and how to go about getting your "car" for your situation.

Dude, Where's My Car?

I remember my first week on campus during my freshman year. My parents unpacked an over-stuffed pickup truck driven by their friend Richard while I unpacked an equally loaded car. It seemed I had brought everything but the kitchen sink to college. What more could I want? What more would I need? Ummmm ... PLENTY!

When my parents and Richard left, so did the truck AND the car! I mean, yeah ... sure, I knew I wasn't going to have a car my first year of college, but it never really dawned on me what it's like to NOT have ANY car at all until I DIDN'T have ANY car at ALL!

Up until this particular time in my life, I hadn't needed to own a car. I still lived at home with my parents and there was always a car available for me to borrow. Now I'm moving two hours away from home and I have NO CAR WHATSOEVER for an entire year! Talk about being unprepared!

After the first three days of walking everywhere on campus (and off) I came to the conclusion that I was going to have to get a car and get one quickly, or I was going to be walking everywhere, regardless of the time, distance, or weather!

This was not a good situation and I was *not* happy.

My Solution

Don't fall for the lie. You don't HAVE to have a car while you're at college. Yes, they're nice to have and very convenient, but don't confuse the issue. *You don't need a car, you just need transportation.* There IS a difference! My suggestion? Find a Super Friend.

During my freshman year I purposely (and strategically) made friends with two people on campus (Miguel and Janay) I knew had cars and would most likely be willing to help me with my transportation needs. They were underclassmen like me and understood the value of having a vehicle while away from home. Both of them were more than happy to help with my transportation problems.

SIDE NOTE: Just so you know, the nicer the car, the less likely it is that the owner of it will let you borrow it. So keep that in mind before befriending the one or two people on campus with the coolest cars.

Now when it comes to my strategic plan for Miguel and Janay, please know that I am **not** saying I "used" these people. Believe me, when I say I befriended them, that's exactly what I did. They are both still good friends of mine today. I have a lot of great memories with them and value their friendship. All I'm saying is, be sure that while you are building your resume of friends at school that you include those with vehicles.

Like the old saying goes, *"If you hang out with nine broke friends, chances are, you're the tenth."* So mix it up a little.

Besides, these new friends with cars will certainly need something you have to offer as well. Who knows? Maybe you could tutor them in math, train them how to work out and eat healthy, help them with their dating skills, laundry, or whatever! So be there for them when you can. **You need them. They need you**. It's a beautiful exchange.

Chapter 8
So You Think You Need a Job?

The second thing I realized shortly after I arrived on campus was that I had no money. I mean NO MONEY. No parents watching TV in the other room where I could just walk in and ask for an extra $20 or so. I mean I had NO MONEY. Now for some of you, that may not be a big deal. Perhaps you have plenty of money and it seems to never end. I don't know … But for the rest of us, money doesn't come quite that easy. We need money and we need it *bad*.

Back home I had a job. I got paid once a week. But now things were different. I was in a new town with new people and I didn't know any of them. If I was going to get money, I was going to have to get a job. Having no job equals having no cash, and with no cash, how was I going to go out on the weekends, go on a date, or even buy things like toothpaste or deodorant? To make matters worse, what's the point of getting a job if I don't have any way of getting to it? (Until I became friends with Miguel and Janay, which didn't happen overnight, I didn't even have transportation!) Talk about going from bad to worse! And this was only the first week of school. Ugh!

My Solution (Part 1): The Money

The money problem is similar to the car scenario I've already discussed in that you must not confuse the issue with the actual problem.

Just because you don't have money, it doesn't mean you need a job. It just means you need money (or what it will buy you).

So what do you do? You already know … find more Super Friends.

Option #1 – The Barter System

The first thing you need to do is to ask yourself what it is you need money for and how much is reasonable to expect on a monthly basis. If you're living on campus and you are already part of the meal plan, then other than some late-night cravings, most of your food should be taken care of. You may want to add-in a little cash for food extras weekly, but it doesn't need to be a lot. (I used to keep peanut butter, jelly and bread in my room. That was plenty.) Throw in a little cash for the occasional party or club outing (cover charges, drinks, gas, gum, etc.), some extra toiletries, and perhaps your monthly phone bill and you should be good.

Now I realize that there may be more to your lifestyle than this, but keep in mind, I'm sharing with you how to get these things with little or no cash and *without* getting a job. So if you choose this route, as I did in college, you're going to have to be a little more strict with your spending habits and a little more strategic with your plan. The strategy I used is similar to the one I discussed concerning my transportation issues: find some fellow students on campus that have the "super power" you need and befriend them.

Now I can hear some of you saying right now, "Wilson ... I can appreciate this Super Friends idea, and I get what you're saying, but I don't wanna borrow money from my friends or seem desperate just to get what I need. That's just not me."

Well that's fine, 'cause I don't want you to do that either! *What I want you to do is think more strategically.*

What is it you need money for? Tutoring? Toiletries? Food? If that's the case, then you don't need money, you need tutoring, toiletries, or food. Do you see what I mean? It's not as difficult as you might think. Let me give you an example of how I used this system while I was in school.

A Deal For A Meal

I'm reminded of this guy I met my freshman year of college. His name was Ross and he became the first member of *my* Super Friends. Ross was in his junior year at our school and his dorm room just happened to be next to mine. Ross was funny, sometimes crazy, and *always* hungry. This guy was eatin' all the time and was constantly offering his supply of extra food to others. (He practically had his own little kitchen right there in his dorm room.)

After getting to know a little about him, I found out that Ross loved music. (He would constantly play "Roxanne" by Sting and sing it sooo loudly that our dorm supervisor would have to threaten to write him up if he didn't turn it and himself down.)

Now of all the things to have, it just so happened that I had an enormous collection of music (I used to DJ back in high school, so I had a lot of music in my own personal collection) and Ross wanted to listen to just about all of it.

So what do you think I did?

I made him a deal. He gave me any extra food he had any time I wanted, and I let him borrow any music I had any time he wanted. I got my hunger fix without buying any food and Ross got his musical fix without buying any music.

(And this was before you could download or purchase a single song at a time from the Internet, so offering him my music saved him from having to buy an entire album just to get the one song he really wanted.)

It was a beautiful thing. I saved him money and he saved me money. Now any money I would've spent on food could be used for something else. Problem solved.

Now you may be saying, "That's great, but my problem isn't food, it's _____." (Fill in the blank with whatever you want.) The object of the problem shouldn't be the focus. The strategy to get it should.

> **Whatever you need or want, one great way of getting it is through befriending others.**

Create your Super Friends. Find something you need that they have and something they need that you have, and exchange services. It's basically a barter system, and it doesn't require cash to work.

Option #2 - Finding Sponsors (Aka "Super Families")

Another way to get money, or to get the stuff you need that money will buy, is by creating a group of friendly sponsors or "Super Families." No, I don't mean getting large sponsors like banks or businesses, but rather, sponsorships from families and friends you already know. These people can help share the load and make your college financial issues practically non-existent.

I'll give you an example: Let's say your monthly phone bill is roughly $90. Instead of asking your parents to pay your phone bill every month (or trying to pay it yourself), find 12 families that will each agree to sponsor you and your phone bill for one month. (Can't find 12? Find six that will sponsor you twice.) These families can come from your church or neighborhood back home, former teachers, relatives, people that work with your parents, etc. Ask each of them to agree to sponsor you by paying your phone bill just one time within the next 12 months. It's just that simple.

Each family is only asked to pay your bill once instead of asking one family to pay it twelve times. And why stop here? This idea can be used for more than just your phone bill.

How about a monthly food sponsor? Gas card sponsor? Care package sponsor?

The list goes on and on … whatever you can think of. Just have them sign up for a particular month and a particular category (food, gas, phone, etc.) and you're well on your way!

ATTENTION! To make this even easier for you, I've created a form you can download from my site for FREE (MJ-Wilson.com) that will help you get started quickly. My form will show your sponsors what you need, how to get it to you, and when. It will also show you ways to keep them informed of your successes due to their support, as well as thank them in various ways without costing you money in the process!

So get to it! Go to my site and download that form! All you have to do is fill in the necessary details and get it to your sponsors! It's just that simple!

Adopt A Grandparent?
When it comes to finding sponsors, there are more people willing to do this than you might think. (Hey! I see you rolling your eyes! Don't do that to me! I'm tellin' you, this works!) Do you know how many older couples there are (especially in churches) that would *love* to have the chance to play the role of "mom & dad" once again in some young person's life just like you? Oftentimes these couples have kids that are grown and finished with college and now they don't feel as needed as they used to. People like this LOVE "adopting kids" for stuff just like this. It allows them to feel necessary again.

And who knows? They may even sign up for more than one category. For example: Perhaps Mr. and Mrs. Doe are willing to pay your phone bill in November *and* send you a gas card in March. Do you see how this works? It's endless.

And why stop at one category or one church or one organization? Get all your expenses covered. And if they signed up to help you your first year, get the same people each year until you graduate! Then invite them to your graduation and the party afterwards and get cash gifts too! Whooo hoooo! This way you won't need to get a job at all while in school and you can spend all your time doing what you went to college to do: getting an education.

So whattaya waiting for???

Go to my site, download the form, find your friendly sponsors and Super Families, and start collecting the goods!

My Solution (Part 2): The Job

Before I even give you my solution about getting a job, let me first say that if you can survive your college years without getting a job (and from what I've shown you above, you can), then you should. The extra time and energy that you would be spending at work could be spent studying, staying healthy (exercising), sleeping (you'll need the rest), or even building friendships. If you still feel you *must* get a job (perhaps you're not as outgoing as others and getting sponsors seems difficult), then please adhere to the following guidelines:

Employment Guidelines While In College

1. Pick a job on campus or nearby.
2. Pick a job that is easy for you to do.
3. Check with your Super Friends for work.
4. Check with your school's administration for work.
5. When you no longer need the job, quit.

---

1) **Make sure the job you apply for and accept is on campus or within walking distance.** This will help you avoid transportation problems (especially in bad weather), traffic, or even high gas prices.

2) **Pick an easy job.** If you can get a job that pays you minimum wage for sitting at a desk signing visitors in and out, vs. a job that pays minimum wage for you to mop floors, stock shelves, and do hard labor, TAKE THE DESK JOB! If the pay is the same or very close, the easier job will be so much easier on you. You'll be less tired when you get off work (so you'll be more likely to study) and you may even be able to read (study) your textbook or complete your class work while you're *at* work. I know this sounds like a "duh" moment, but you'd be surprised how many people will apply anywhere for a job and accept anything they get.

3) **Check with your Super Friends or Super Families.** Perhaps one or more of them works somewhere on or near campus that is hiring and can help you get a job with them. Or maybe they know one of your professors or school administrators and can put in a good word for you for a campus position. This resource can be very useful, so don't forget to check with them while searching for some work.

4) **Check with your school's administration to see if there is work available on campus.** Several schools offer work right on campus that either pays money or gives discounts on other campus items. These types of jobs are great because they keep you on campus, meaning no transportation is needed and you won't need a car or have to pay for gas! Besides, being on campus will also allow you to get to know more people at your school and will increase the odds of you being allowed to study while at work since you work at the actual facility that's educating you.

5) **Finally, if and when the time comes that you no longer need the job, be done with it!** Put in your two weeks' notice and move on. You have the rest of your life to work. Enjoy your college experience now while you can. It will go by much quicker than you think. Believe me.

Chapter 9
The Super Friends

Due to all my talk about the Super Friends in the previous chapter, I thought it would only be right to share with you a little about *my* first group of Super Friends. It all took place during my freshman year of college.

I was having a difficult time adjusting to my new life ... my "college life." I didn't just need some friends, I needed some *super* friends.

> **As crazy as it may sound, I was 19 years old and had never had to do my own laundry until now.**

When you're the youngest of four kids like I was growing up, laundry isn't exactly something your parents expect you to do. So as simple as it may be, it was foreign to me. I also found it difficult to get around on campus (no car, remember?), keep up with my customary exercise/workout routine, or even find someone to go to the movies with. I was a wreck! I felt outta place and outta friends and this was dangerous. The longer this feeling persisted, the more likely it was for me to want to transfer to a school back home, or drop out of school altogether simply because of depression, loneliness, or poor life skills. I had to do something and do it fast. So the search was on!

Lucky for me, as I began my search I realized I didn't have to look far. As a matter of fact, all but two of my Super Friends were staying within 20 yards of my dorm suite and were a perfect match for what I needed.

My Super Friends consisted of Ross, Miguel, Janay, Ben, Brian and Christina.

Ross you already know about. He's the guy I spoke of who exchanged his food for my music.

I also had **Miguel** and **Janay**. As I mentioned before, both had transportation available for me at all times. Miguel was a very funny guy and a bit of a ladies man (at least in his mind he was) and Janay was very soft spoken and a bit of a "Southern Belle". Either one of them would drive me anywhere for anything at anytime.

(By the way, be sure to pick <u>two</u> friends with cars and not just one in case one is using their car at the time you need it.)

Then there was **Ben**. He was overly scholastic and a gentleman's gentleman. Very well-spoken, well-versed in theater and the arts, had a booming bass voice (he performed on campus for our school), and could keep a dorm room so clean yet comfortable that his suite seemed more like a home than a dorm. He always had extra cash around whenever you needed it and didn't mind sharing it with his friends, which was a huge help!

Listen Outside The Box

Having Ben around also encouraged me to expand my mind when it came to the music and movies I normally consumed. Before I met Ben, I was strictly a Hip-Hop and R&B type of guy. (I grew up listening to RUN-DMC and Michael Jackson.) However, after hanging out with him and gaining a new appreciation for other art forms, I soon found myself listening to anything from Frank Sinatra to Mozart as well. What a change!

Ben not only helped to make my college experience more interesting and fun, he also encouraged me to have an open mind about other people and their customs, which made surviving college *much* easier. He was very helpful and turned out to be a great, genuine friend.

The Big Man On Campus

Then there was **Brian**. He was a big, muscular, beefy guy that had a streak of Italian in him that made him a lot of fun to be around anytime anyone disagreed with him. (He could argue in the most amazing, blunt, and lawyer-like ways.) He worked out in his own makeshift gym on campus religiously and encouraged me to do the same. Not only was he a great guy for helping me get in shape and stay healthy, but having him around was like having my own personal bodyguard. *The guy was huge. Nobody messed with him.* And since he and I would hang out a lot, nobody messed with me. I loved it.

Brian was definitely an asset to my college experience and certainly helped make it easier for me. What a great, great friend.

Mother Goose

Finally, there was **Christina**. She was my "mom away from home." She would take care of my laundry, run errands for me, or help clean my room. (She even made a bowl of chicken soup for me once, complete with crackers and a damp, warm cloth for my forehead during that time I mentioned earlier when I had the flu.) Her mothering instincts and subtle ways made my college life more like home life and so much more bearable when things were tough. I still keep in touch with her to this day. Due to Christina's "Super Power" and the others' powers as well, I believe you can see why these six friends of mine not only became great friends, but *Super Friends*, too.

Chapter 10
Old Friends vs. New Friends

One of the first things you'll notice about college life is the battle (usually in your mind or heart) for where to place your loyalty when it comes to your new friends vs. your old friends.

Many times we spend our last summer before going off to college with our best friends from high school. Several of these friends we've known since grade school and we have formed bonds with them that will last a lifetime. Now here we are in college with an entirely new group of friends and soon to be new memories as well. It seems the closer we get to our new friends, the further away we get from our old ones.

To some of you, that's no big deal. It's just time to move on. For others though, it's really hard. There's a sense of loyalty that's being stretched (or so it seems) and along with it, even a feeling of guilt to some degree.

Best Friends Forever? (Probably Not ... But Maybe)
What do you do when you no longer want to go home every weekend because you'd rather stay on campus with your new friends? Or what do you do when you don't mind going home to visit, but you wanna take one or more of your new friends home with you? Is that okay?

Is it normal to feel a little guilty as if you're not being faithful to the friendships you've spent a lifetime on back home? The ones you've spent years cultivating? Of course it is! And don't sweat it either. It's just a new chapter in your life.

You don't have to ditch your old friends or "quit" them just because you have new ones.

Let me just point something out right now. Fred Reeder, the guy who is editing this very book that you are reading, is one of my best friends. He and I met in the 5th grade and we're *still* friends to this day. And just so you know, we

DIDN'T go to the same college. (In case you're wondering, Fred attended Miami University in Oxford, Ohio.)

So believe me, it's not as big of a deal as you might think. Just because you don't see your old friends every day anymore, it doesn't mean you're losing them. With the advent of social networks like Facebook and Skype, maintaining old friendships from a distance is now easier than ever. Besides, who knows what technology we'll have in the years to come? It will only get easier.

I will tell you though, the old friends back home may think differently, especially if they're still *back home*.

In other words, if your old friends back home didn't go off to college somewhere or move out on their own to a new town with a new job, then they're not meeting anyone new (like you are) and rather than experiencing a new life with new friends in a new town, they're experiencing a sense of loss from their old life, with their old friends in their hometown. *Your* hometown.

This is where they can become "sticky."

You go home and they'll wanna do everything with you the entire time you're there and they may not want to "share you" with anyone else (hence the term "sticky"), especially not with any of your new friends you bring home from college. They may even complain that "You've changed" or "You're just not the same anymore." If they tell you that, they're probably right (or at least I hope they are!)

You HAVE changed. You AREN'T the same. You've grown up, and they need to as well.

My Solution

Why did I share all of that information about the sticky friends with you? What does all of that have to do with you surviving and graduating from college? Because if you aren't aware of what's actually happening to you and you're not prepared for it, you will mistake their "stickiness" for your own lack of loyalty and faithfulness.

Once this happens, watch out ... The first time you have one problem away from home, one really bad day at your new school, one fight with your new boyfriend or girlfriend on campus, you're gonna wanna run right back home to your old friends and your old ways simply because it is what you're used to and it will (if only temporarily) make you feel very comfortable in an otherwise, uncomfortable situation.

BELIEVE ME. This happens more than you think!

Students find themselves in this scenario and end up transferring to a local school back home, or dropping out altogether and going to work back home just to satisfy this insecurity and misunderstanding. In the end it's just a little drama and a matter of growing up.

Don't let a lack of maturity on their part and a little misunderstanding on yours cause you to add another semester (or year) to your graduation date by transferring schools or dropping out temporarily. And you definitely don't wanna let something like this knock you outta school altogether!

Remember, this book is about *surviving* college and making the most of your experience while you're there. Your goal is not only to *stay* in school and graduate (which is a big enough goal already), but to graduate *on time*. So stay put! And don't get stuck on your sticky friends.

Chapter 11
Parties, Alcohol and Sex

Before I even start on this problem, let me say one thing right now:

> ### It is not my role or place to tell you what to do concerning parties, alcohol or sex, and I won't do so in this book.

ATTENTION! If you're a parent or teacher reading this book, don't worry ... I'm NOT going to suggest your son, daughter or students start or stop participating in any of these activities. Whatever you or they believe and live according to is really none of my business.

My goal is to simply inform them that if such topics are not dealt with properly (from a scholastic viewpoint) that these topics, when in full fruition, may jeopardize their chances of graduation.

To ignore them would be asinine. They DO exist and they ARE prevalent on most, if not all campuses (sometimes even on campuses where they're forbidden).

So believe me, when it comes to surviving college and dealing with the things that can keep you from graduating, these three topics are right at the top for sure. So let's explore how they can become a problem and then how you can deal with them successfully so that you don't become a dropout, flunkout, transfer statistic and/or a graduate casualty.

New Kid On The Block
As I've stated before, you're in a new school in a new town with new friends. Everything's new again ... even you (if you wanna be). And that's where the problems come in. With new beginnings come new opportunities, and along with those opportunities comes the power to choose whether you stay true to your roots or try something new.

Unfortunately, a lot of students try something new with no regard (or perhaps, no real understanding) of what they're really risking by jumping into whatever "opportunity" comes their way. (It's one thing to experience new ideas, new cultures, new friends. It's another to just throw all caution out the window and do whatever you want just because you can.)

A word of advice: *Use your new freedom wisely or it will use you foolishly.*

> ### Nobody said when you go to college you have to become something you're not or do things you don't feel comfortable with.

I can appreciate the new freedom you now have as an adult and college student, but you should, too. Seriously. *Appreciate it.* Don't take advantage of it in a negative way. You've now been entrusted to live like an adult, so do it.

Remember, the goal is to survive college, not become a casualty of it. If your new *free*dom is costing you your education, *then it's not free.* You're a paying customer. And you'll pay for it the rest of your life if you're not careful.

Girls Gone Wild! (Or Should I Say Students?)

I can't begin to tell you how many young girls I've known over the years who lived a very reserved, stable life while in junior high and high school only to go off to college, party like a rockstar every chance they got, and end up dropping out before or during their sophomore year due to an unexpected pregnancy. Or how many young athletes I've known who have gone off to college with big plans of becoming the first person from their family to graduate, or even bigger, making it into professional sports after they graduate, only to fall prey to binge drinking and excessive partying, thus dropping out of school due to flunking out.

Enjoy college, yes. But don't regret it.

Who Do You Think You Are? My Dad?

Now hear me out. I am not here to preach to you or act like your mom or dad. If you are sexually active or like to party every weekend, that's up to you. You're most likely an adult now, so you can (or should be able to) make those decisions on your own. My advice to stay true to your foundational belief system (at least for now) is not based upon a religious belief or lack of one on my part. I am simply advising you that if you have lived a certain way for the majority of your life and then you go to college and switch everything up, you are greatly and sadly increasing your chances of becoming another college dropout statistic.

My Solution

If you wanna go crazy and experience all that college life has to offer, that's up to you. But if you feel you must do this, *I highly recommend you do it in moderation and with understanding.* Remember, the goal is to graduate and graduate on time. You didn't go to college to party ... you can do that without it. You went to college to get an education. So get it!

> **Don't blow it all in one night by being in the wrong place at the wrong time and regretting it for the rest of your life.**

A general rule I live by is simply this: *"If you don't have peace, don't do it."* That has served me well over the years. It will serve you well, too. You know you better than anyone. Be true to yourself. Remember, you're the one who has to live with the consequences your decisions bring.

Am I saying you can't or shouldn't party, drink or have sex? Like I stated earlier, that's really none of my business. Those decisions are up to you and the foundational beliefs you've been raised to trust and embrace up to this point. What you do is really *your* business. Now you may be saying, "I realize they're my decisions Wilson, but do you think I *should* participate in any of these activities?" If this is you, I recommend that you seek people in your life that you trust and admire (like a parent, relative, counselor, pastor or friend) and ask for their advice or opinion concerning these topics. They should be able to help steer you in the right direction. I will, however, be glad to share with you a few statistics[3] that may be able to help you in your decision-making process.

Alcohol

- **Underage Drinking** (under 21 years of age) in most states is punishable by law with a fine ranging from $250-$1000 and possible imprisonment ranging from 30-180 days.

- **Fake ID's** (typically used by college students to purchase alcohol or gain admission into an establishment serving liquor) in most states warrant a fine ranging from $250-$1000 and possible imprisonment ranging from 30 days to 6 months.

---

[3] These statistics were based on research I found throughout many books and websites (such as the Center for Disease Control, state laws, etc.). And these laws/stats may vary from state and region, as well as from year to year. As with anyone or anything, "results may vary." These stats are not etched in stone. I simply placed them here to make you aware of the "facts" (and I use that word loosely) about these topics.

- **Driving Under the Influence (DUI)** or Operating a Vehicle while under the Influence (OVI) in most states is punishable by law with a fine ranging from $250-$1000 and a mandatory 3 days in jail with a possibility of up to 6 months imprisonment, as well as a possible suspension of driver's license ranging from 6 months to 3 years.

Sex

- **Sexually Transmitted Disease (STD)** – 1 in 4 college students has one.

- **Sexually Transmitted Infection (STI)** – Roughly 19 million newly transmitted infections occur each year with almost half occurring among 15-24 year-olds.

- **Unplanned Pregnancy** – More than one-third of all unplanned pregnancies occur with unmarried women in their twenties.

- **Drop Out Rate** – About 60% of women who have children after enrolling in college fail to finish their degree.

OUCH! That Hurt!

Just so we're clear, all colleges have substance abuse and underage drinking policies[4]. (These policies help protect the colleges from lawsuits, among other things.) And although each college varies in its disciplinary measures, the penalties are *harsh*. They are nothing to play with. (Some schools will suspend you just for being charged with a DUI … even if you're not convicted!) And that's just the suspension. Students who are suspended from a typical college/university can also lose tuition, financial aid, athletic eligibility, internship, residence hall costs/fees, and even study abroad eligibility (and these are just the ones I can think of off the top of my head!)

All of this, not to mention, *time*. Many students find they have to sit out a semester or even one full academic year, only to start all over again the following year. Ouch!

So keep this in mind while you're planning that big toga-keg party with all your friends.

It Is What It Is

Sex, regardless of your viewpoint of how it is or is not to be handled, can play a major, *major* role in the success or failure of your college survival. Just reread

---

[4] Obviously, any form of illegal drug is a bad idea altogether. If you are even *remotely* linked to these in any way (even if you don't use them), you could find yourself in much deeper trouble than I have time or space to list in this book. Nothing good will come out of you participating in any illegal drug activity whatsoever. So *please* avoid it and them.

those statistics I listed earlier. It's so much more likely that you won't finish school if you have a baby on the way, and certainly much more difficult (and expensive) if you wake up one day with a sexual disease. (Not to mention the emotional stress and social strain that can cause.)

So if you are sexually active, or if you plan to be during your college experience, please take the necessary measures to ensure that all activity is as safe and responsible as possible for all parties involved. Remember, *you are rare*. There is nobody else like you in the world. We (your family, friends, the world, me) want you around, happy and healthy for years to come, sharing your knowledge, talent and new expertise that only comes with that diploma you so desperately desire and so earnestly deserve.

(I kinda sounded like a caring father there, didn't I? See ... I told ya I care!)

And just so you know, YES, I AM AWARE that it IS POSSIBLE to drink and not drive, get drunk and not get injured, have sex without getting pregnant (or a disease), and also actually return to school at a later date and graduate after being suspended or getting pregnant OR dropping out! YES. I DO KNOW THIS. And YES, it IS possible.

But it's not likely.

When it comes to parties, activities, and other crazy events, please realize you have the rest of your life to participate in any or all of them. These activities have been around forever and they're not going anywhere. BUT, the opportunity to go to college and get a degree is much more rare and fleeting. If you drop out for any reason, the odds of you going back and finishing aren't nearly as good as they would be had you just stayed in to begin with. (Believe me ... check the research!)

During your first year of college, especially your first few months, you have sooo much going on that is demanding your attention and mental abilities that the last thing you need to do is add more stress to your life by changing your foundational beliefs and ideals (whatever they may be).

Remember, what got you here will keep you here (at least for now). So chill out. You've got plenty of time to "learn the ropes" and experience college life. For now, try to focus on getting your basics intact (like reading and doing what I suggest in this book!)

Besides, if you party the right way, you'll not only enjoy and remember your college experience, but you'll be around to do more of it.

Chapter 12
The Problem with Hazing

If there's one thing that comes to mind when I think of "the college life," it's the crazy memories that come with it. Ask any college graduate about the craziest thing they ever did while in college and they may have to decline and politely offer to tell you the second craziest thing they ever did because whatever they did that resides in first place is just too embarrassing or wrong to tell.

Make A Memory, Not A Permanent Record
Although these memories make for great stories around a campfire or when you're older reliving the "good ole days," please realize that *there's a difference between making a memory and making a mistake.* It's one thing to have a little fun, but it's another thing to end up in the county jail overnight (or prison). The last thing you wanna do is add a permanent record to your resumé while you're trying to add a degree to it. Twenty years from now, whichever you decide, either one will still be with you.

So use your brain for more than a late-night dare or last-minute challenge. What starts out as innocent fun in the beginning can easily turn into a horrible tragedy in the end.

My Solution

Probably the worst-case scenarios of a memory becoming a mistake reside within the hazing process that seems to be so prevalent throughout many colleges, regardless of how much they work to prohibit it.

Hazing: humiliating and sometimes dangerous initiation rituals, especially as imposed on college students seeking membership in a fraternity/sorority, or other on-campus organization.

Now before I go any further, please HEAR ME NOW and realize that although hazing often involves on-campus groups (from the Greek life or sports to marching bands and beyond), I am NOT saying that all fraternities, sororities, or other such groups participate in this type of activity. On the contrary, some fraternities and sororities (as well as other on-campus groups) are of the utmost prestige and pride and would never encourage nor condone such practices.

However …

> ***Many students have found themselves on the wrong side of a suspension, expulsion, or lawsuit due to improper practices involving the hazing of other students.***

What often starts out as a harmless prank (usually due to some type of initiation process or pledging) can easily turn into a stupid (and dangerous) act that leaves several people hurt in the process, whether physically, academically, or emotionally. Besides this, it also brings very negative press to you, your organization, and school.

Before you plan, participate, and enact any idea or event for the sake of "a little fun, tradition, and memories" please ask yourself the following questions:

- Is what I'm about to do illegal?

- Is there a possibility that someone will get hurt or abused (emotionally or physically)?

- Am I, or current/active members of my group, refusing to participate with our new members and do exactly the same thing we are asking them to do?

- Would I have any reservations describing what I am about to do to my school administrators, parents or local police?

- Would I object to this activity/event being recorded (video) for the school website, newspaper or local TV?

- Is this something that could result in my suspension, expulsion, or worse?

If you answered any of these questions with a "yes" then I HIGHLY recommend that you do **NOT** participate in your activity/event whatsoever! I also recommend that you inform others that may be involved as well. And if you feel your activity/event falls in a grey area that is not so black and white, and you're unsure about its legality, I recommend you contact your school's administration and seek their advice and approval before going any further with your plan.

And please, please don't let your pride and ego get in the way. I can hear some of you now … "Oh there's no *waaay* I'm gonna ask my school if I can do this! Are you nuts Wilson??? What do you think I am? Some kind of idiot?" And if that's your response, then I think I've just proven my point. If there's really *no waaay* you're asking, then what is it your trying to get away with?

Listen, I know you wanna fit in and be one of the guys/girls, and I know the group you're wanting to join may be everything you want, but please remember why you came to school in the first place: to get an education. Anything else is just extra.

If you wanna party, that's up to you. But you can do that *without* college AND without a permanent record.

Leave the illegal activities to the criminals. It's not your style anyway. If it were, you wouldn't be *here* and you wouldn't be reading this survival guide.

You're different.

You're better than that.

Do the right thing and stay focused. Do you hear me? STAY FOCUSED!

SIDE NOTE: After reading over this book one last time before sending it off to the publisher, I got to this section and thought it would be a good place to put an example or two of some actual hazing experiences that went terribly wrong, in hopes of convincing you to steer clear of such activity. But after reading several cases (many of which were far more horrendous than I had imagined), I have decided against it simply because I do not want to glorify any such acts or spawn any copycat scenarios. Our country's history is littered with example after example, unfortunately, *and some are very disturbing.*

However, I do think it is appropriate to list a few of the general guidelines that most schools and states enforce in regard to hazing. These policies and consequences may vary from state to state or school to school, but for the most part the following guidelines and laws are prevalent in each. And as you can see, hazing is no laughing matter. With so many bullying cases being made known today via the Internet and other social media, the fines are becoming more and more severe.

Being guilty of such a crimes can be so damaging to your college career (and life, for that matter) that you may never live it down, let alone, finish school. And if by chance you are accused of hazing, yet found innocent, the time and court costs alone are enough to wipe out your chances of graduating. So please, *please* take my advice and this section seriously. Hazing is not only a serious offense, it can be downright deadly.

COMMON HAZING GUIDELINES & LAWS

College/University Guidelines

Rules – Each institution shall provide a program for the enforcement of hazing rules and shall adopt appropriate penalties for violations of these rules to be administered by the institution.

Individual Penalties – These may include the imposition of fines, the withholding of diplomas or transcripts depending upon your compliance with the rules or payment of fines and the imposition of probation, suspension or dismissal.

Group Penalties – In the case of any organization that authorizes hazing in blatant disregard of such rules, penalties may also include the cancellation of that organization to operate on campus property or to otherwise operate under the sanction or recognition of the institution.

Individual and Group Penalties – These rules apply to acts conducted on or off campus whenever such acts are deemed to constitute hazing.

Basic State Laws

Imprisonment – A person who has been convicted of an offense may be sentenced to imprisonment for a term anywhere from a few days up to a year (or more depending upon the severity of the crime).

Fines – A person who has been convicted of an offense may be sentenced to pay a fine anywhere from a few hundred dollars to a few thousand (or more depending upon the severity of the crime).

I'm not just trying to keep you in college and out of jail, but quite possibly, out of the grave prematurely. It really is *that* serious.

ATTENTION! Before moving into the next chapter of this book concerning whether to join fraternities and sororities, etc., I want to (once more) make something PERFECTLY CLEAR. I am by NO MEANS suggesting that *all* fraternities, sororities, or other on-campus clubs are involved in hazing of any kind. Some are <u>strongly</u> against it and will have nothing to do with it.

Please understand, some of these on-campus groups are absolutely *phenomenal* to be a part of and something to be proud of, long after you've graduated and moved on.

However, when hazing *does* occur, oftentimes an on-campus group such as the ones we've listed are typically involved in some way. So please be aware of exactly what group it is you are considering pledging, auditioning, or applying for and where they stand on such issues. I truly believe if you are well educated and in the know, there will be no reason you can't find the perfect group for you … One that is safe, legal, and a privilege to become a member of.

Now, having said all that, whattaya say we move on to these beloved groups we hold so dear to our hearts and decide which one, if any, is for you? (Smile.)

Chapter 13

On-Campus Clubs: Should You Join Them?

To join or not to join, really is the question. The funny thing is, it seems most college students who pledge a fraternity or sorority or apply for membership within a campus club don't really even know why they're doing it. I mean, *I know why they do it*: they usually do it 'cause they wanna party, or meet guys/girls, or have a sense of belonging, or because one or more of their family members was a member. And to be honest, there's really nothing wrong with these reasons. They all have their place and merit. But like I said, *I know why they do it* … my question is, "Do they?" Do you?

If you're going to join any group on campus (or anywhere else for that matter), you should know exactly why. What is it you expect from it? What benefit is it to you to be a part of this organization?

And don't think I'm suggesting you *not* join. I'm being very sincere when I ask of what benefit it will be to you. Think of it this way … If you're only joining a fraternity to meet girls, then my question to you is, "Is the fraternity your pledging good at helping its members meet girls?" Cause if it's not, then you're not going to be satisfied with it. Or to you ladies … Do you wanna join a sorority to create a bond with other girls on campus and create a sense of sisterhood? Or simply just to meet other girls and guys? If so, is the sorority you're pledging any good at doing this? If not, then you're not going to be satisfied with it, either.

Time After Time

What does this have to do with surviving college and graduating? Plenty! If you spend hours and hours pledging an organization or participating in activities that consume your time and energy but do not satisfy your wants, needs, or expectations, you will soon become frustrated and tired (more mentally than physically, although it can be physical as well) and mistake this feeling with other feelings … feelings that say, "I don't like this school. Nobody 'gets' me here. I think I should transfer to another school or go back home. I'm just not happy here."

Remember, the goal is to survive (graduate, and graduate on time). The odds of this happening become worse when you are not pleased with your social life on campus.

Besides, these activities are no joke. Some of them take *a lot of time*. Time that could be spent studying, resting, making new friends, or even pledging or applying for membership in a different organization on campus. You don't wanna be halfway through your sophomore or junior year and come to the realization you should've joined some other group and now it's either too late to join or if you do, you're gonna have to start all over again.

Please realize, *anything that adds time to your college experience adds time to your graduation date.* In other words, you wanna graduate and graduate on time. You don't wanna be like me and take six (college) years to get a four-year degree, stretched out over an eight-year period. It only delays your entrance into your new career while adding money onto your student loans. Not to mention, it also delays your new pay scale.

The Flip Side
Just so you don't think I'm against you joining any of the groups we've mentioned, or those like them, I want to give you another point of view before making your decision.

I know of several friends and even former students of mine who have joined fraternities, sororities, and other on-campus groups and have found them to be one of the highlights of their lives. Many of them have formed bonds (like a "brotherhood" or "sisterhood") that will stay with them the rest of their lives.

And talk about social networking! You join a fairly large and active group and you may have just become part of a nationwide (or even global) network that will have your back wherever you go for the rest of your life! Now *that's* impressive.

I know of friends of mine who joined certain fraternities/sororities that are well connected nationwide. Any time any of them travel across the U.S., they contact that chapter or group within the city they're going to and let them know of their future arrival. Many of these groups, although the current people involved may never have personally met these past members, will treat these members like royalty whenever they're in town. They'll show them the ropes or possibly offer them a place to stay, or hang out with them and show them a good time. It's like having a family across the nation (or in some cases, across the globe) to spend time with, get to know, and make memories with, while feeling safe and even valued.

So believe me, membership *can* have its privileges. It just depends on what type of group you join and their overall status and impact around the world. Certainly something to think about.

My Solution

It is my belief that hospitals are for sick people, parachutes are for skydivers and flowerbeds are for flowers.

What do I mean by all of this?

Well, when it comes to joining an on-campus organization, my question is, "Is it for you? Is it where you belong? Do you need it or does it need you?" If so, then by all means go for it. You will most likely enjoy the benefits that it will bring to you and your college experience and it will in turn enjoy what you bring to it. I only ask that if you do decide to join any group, please research it first. Find out what its successes and failures (if any) are. Find out if it does what it says it can or if it's truly what you need. Because if it's not for you, you'll be like a person wearing a parachute who never plans on skydiving: You'll look awkward and feel awkward. The chute, instead of helping you stay alive, will only weigh you down – and eventually will become a nuisance.

If it's not for you, not only will it waste your time, but you'll waste its time as well. It reminds me of a friend of mine who used to always say, "The only thing worse than being divorced is wishing you were." Whether you agree with that statement or not, I think you get the point. You certainly don't wanna be a part of a group that you wish you weren't. You'll just become dead weight to them and they'll just become something that takes all your valuable time. Do this long enough and you'll both actually begin to resent each other, and that's when things can really get ugly (and you don't want that).

So choose wisely.

> **On this wonderful planet we call Earth, we have many renewable resources, but time isn't one of them.**

Once it's gone, it's gone.

And yours will be, too.

Chapter 14
Why You Definitely Need a College Roadmap

Why Aren't We Moving?

While attending the University of Rio Grande, my sister Sherri and a friend of hers, Makoto (an Asian exchange student from Japan with a strong Japanese accent and great sense of humor), decided to take a weekend road trip to Fort Wayne, Indiana. They had just finished a brutal week of studying for exams and Makoto wanted to get away and visit some of his friends from Japan who were staying in Fort Wayne over the weekend for a wrestling tournament. My sister thought this was a great idea and agreed to go with him.

She quickly packed her things and met Makoto out front in the dorm parking lot. As she shut the car door, she looked over at Makoto, waiting for him to start the car and go. After a few seconds (which seemed like an eternity), she asked him,

"Is there something wrong? What are you waiting for? Why aren't we moving?"

To which Makoto looked over at her and with the most sincere, most innocent, heartfelt reply, spoken in a very strong Japanese accent with a slight smile, said, "You have map?"

(Yes, you read that right. He didn't say, "Do you have a map we can use?" but literally said, "You have map?")

My sister burst out into laughter and once she calmed down enough to speak, she looked at him and said, "You mean to tell me you want me to drive from Rio Grande, Ohio to Fort Wayne, Indiana with you and you don't even have a map or directions? Are you serious? You gotta be kidding me!"

Well he *was* serious and he *wasn't* kidding. He didn't have a map *or* directions. And keep in mind, this was before the Internet and tracking systems, so without a map or directions, you were setting yourself up to be lost quickly.

To make a long story short, my sister ended up going to a local gas station and buying a U.S. road map for directions. They successfully made it to Fort Wayne and back safely and on time. As a matter of fact, it has been one of the best road trips and memories she's ever made. She has no regrets and neither does Makoto.

It's a funny story, but one that could've turned out much worse.

What if their destination would've been something more important than simply wanting to visit some friends in Indiana? What if the trip they were taking had a strict timeline attached to it and each day that passed the expected arrival date cost them more and more money? What if it would've cost them opportunities that were only available during a specific window of time? Would it matter more then?

If you want to graduate from college (and graduate on time), how will you get from where you are to where you want to be without a map?

A lot of students never make it to their destination (they don't graduate) and many others take the long way to get there (graduating one, two, or even three years later than what they should have), costing them thousands of more dollars (and student loan interest) as well as costing them possible job opportunities.

Remember, my first degree took me six (college) years to get, stretched out over an eight-year period and I should've completed it in four! I ended up paying more money, losing more time, and missing out on four years' worth of teaching and salary. I know what I'm talking about! So don't be like most of us who made the mistake of making the trip without a map, or like Makoto and waiting until the last minute to find your way. You may not be as lucky as he was to find someone like my sister to help you.

My Solution

First of all, if at all possible, get your "college roadmap" before you even go to college. This is something that ideally you should have by the end of your junior year in high school. (Notice I said "ideally." In all reality, you probably are just starting college or already have and that's okay. I can still help you get on course. Just be sure to follow my lead.)

The first thing you'll need to do is create your map. And although this will be similar to the vision you created at the beginning of this book, it is not the same. It is different and should be completed fully.

If you want help with this just go to my website (MJ-Wilson.com) and download one for FREE! (See ... I told you I care about you! I'm on YOUR side, remember?) It will give you a great start and save you some time. Besides, why reinvent the wheel, right? However, if you still choose to create your own college roadmap, that's fine, too. Just be sure you include the following:

College Roadmap Guidelines

- **START DATE** (month/year you plan to start or started college)

- **GRADUATION DATE** (month/year you plan to graduate)

- **A FOUR-YEAR PLAN** (or longer, depending upon your major) of all the courses you need to take and by what time you need to take them (so as to qualify for necessary programs that exist within your major). An admission counselor or advisor at your college should be able to show you a rough idea of what courses you'll need. (They should already have these planned out because anyone wanting to complete their major and graduate will have to take the same courses respective to that field to do it. The only exception would be transfer students who may be able to take fewer courses depending upon what transfers.)

- **SUMMER PLANS** that will boost your chances of success (like working as a summer intern for a future employer instead of going back home and delivering pizzas at your old high school job) for each summer during your college experience, and more.

Although I can help you along the way, I recommend that you have your map reviewed or tweaked by a trusted individual who will know what they're talking about because they've "been there, done that."

And although I realize that your school's guidance counselor may be the perfect person for this and more than willing to do so, please realize counselors most likely have about a zillion other students they're working with as well, so you may not get the attention you truly need.

You may want to seek the help of someone else instead: possibly an aunt/uncle who graduated from college, a current or former teacher you trust, maybe your parents (if they're college graduates), a professor one of your older siblings or friends knows, or possibly even a professor at your current school if you are already enrolled in college. These people will be able to point out some things you may have overlooked and help you stay on track and accountable for your goals.

Whomever you get, I do not recommend that you get help from someone who hasn't attended college and *finished*. They will most likely not be aware of all the "ins and outs" necessary to make your map successful. If they were, they probably would've graduated themselves. Now I don't mean that in a harsh manner. I'm being very serious. This isn't a joke. We're talking about your future career, thousands of dollars, and the most valuable asset you possess: time. So please hear me out on this one. Get someone who has successfully graduated and knows what they're talking about! Okay? Good! (Smile.)

Chapter 15
How To Find Good Professors

As I mentioned previously, not all of us are fortunate enough to have someone help us along our journey like my sister helped Makoto with his. We may have to be a little more strategic ... more savvy. So that's just what we'll be.

However, if you did find someone already to help you create your map based upon the options I listed previously, I'm still gonna need you to find two more "passengers" to take along on your journey. Think of these passengers like your navigation system. They'll help guide you through your journey (college experience) once you've given them your road map (where you are and where you are going) to your final destination (graduation).

And by the way, these passengers we're looking for are not your classmates, family or friends.

They're your professors.

But not just any professors! You want good, trustworthy professors. And these professors don't necessarily need to be *your* professors, either (as in, they don't necessarily have to teach a class that you attend), although it does help.

And why do I want you to find two? Because this will allow you to get more than one viewpoint on the same subject or situation. And if you can, get one female and one male. This will allow for a more varied understanding and overall viewpoint. Just be sure these professors are credible, trustworthy professors. I can't emphasize enough how important it is to find two that you can trust to share your dreams, ideas, and failures with. That is, trust them within reason ...

> ### Please realize they don't need to become your therapist or hear about "that one time at band camp."

Just find two professors (and I mean like in the first three to four weeks) and begin a healthy mentor/student relationship. Ask these professors if they would be willing to somewhat "guide" you through your courses and college decisions.

Now please realize I am not asking you to ask these professors to become your "college advisor." That is an actual position most colleges already have someone hired to do, and you will have one, or already have one assigned to you. However, that's the problem; they're *assigned* to you. You didn't pick them and they didn't pick you. *It's their job.* You could be very important to them (I've had some wonderful advisors in my time) or you could also just be another number on their spreadsheet.

And don't get me wrong. I'm not saying these advisors won't do a good job, but what they're paid to do for you and what I'm wanting the two trustworthy professors to do for you aren't the same thing. These advisors will advise you on how to sign up for a class or let you know when a course deadline is for withdrawal, etc., but that's not what I'm talking about.

I want you to find two professors that you can share the bigger picture with. You know, stuff like, "Hello Professor X. I have a question for you. I have the option of going home over the summer (two hours away) and working a part-time job or staying here on/near campus and working a summer program for course credit. If you were in my shoes with my financial situation, what would you do? What do you recommend?" Or maybe something like, "Professor So-and-So, I'm thinking of changing my major from Y to Z. I heard that Y no longer is in demand like it used to be and I don't want to be jobless when I graduate. What are your thoughts?"

If they say they're too busy or give you some reason why they don't think that advising you is a good idea, then they're right ... it won't be a good idea (not with them at least) and you should just move on to other professors. Once you find the right ones, see them for their value and worth that is in your life for this season and make the most of it! Begin to see them like a gold mine and you are the miner. Get in there and get all the nuggets of wisdom and understanding you can.

Just as I am sharing this book and all my wisdom with you, so too, can these professors share with you their experiences, mistakes, successes and failures. You'll know when you have the right ones because the right ones will see it as a privilege and an honor to step into your life and share theirs. So keep that in mind.

I know a lot of professors. Some are tired of their job and wish they could afford to quit. Others LOVE what they do and see every day as a chance to guide a young soul like yours around the pitfalls and traps of everyday life.

Find them.

LISTEN to them.

And celebrate their value while you can.

They'll change your life for the better, demand more of you than you do of yourself, and keep you grounded. Besides, you'll miss them when you're gone.

Trust me.

My Solution

There are three possible solutions that I have found work pretty well for this problem and they are very practical for what you'll need. Choose one (or more) and make it happen.

Big Brother, Big Sister
As for finding two trustworthy professors, one approach you might use is to find a junior or senior student on your college campus now whom you trust and admire and ask them if they could recommend one or more professors that might be willing to help you. Since these students have been on campus longer than you they should know the ropes a little better and might be able to save you some time.

Good Vibrations
Another approach is to simply get a feel and vibe for any of the professors you currently have for class and see if you click with any of them. These will be the ones that you seem to just "get" and they "get" you. Be sure they aren't just impressive though. You want to choose professors who truly seem to care about their students' well-being and not just the ones that you think are cool or good-looking. (Yes ... I know how some of you think!)

Keep in mind that as the year goes on, you will have different professors. The ones you have for the next quarter or semester may click with you even better than the ones you have now and choose at first. If this is the case (and the new professors are willing to help you), you may want to switch to a new one (or more) as the year goes on.

However, I don't recommend switching often. Try to stick with the same "passengers" as much as possible during your journey. This will help ensure your journey is smooth and consistent and will increase your odds of graduating *on time.*

Help Wanted? Inquire Within

Finally, you may want to check with the college admissions department (or any department designed to help facilitate incoming freshmen or transfer students) and inquire about any programs they may offer to do exactly what it is you're looking for: guidance! Just beware, as I've stated before, there's a difference between someone being assigned to you (where you risk becoming just a name and number) and someone who gets you and truly wants to help. Be sure that whomever you choose, that person has your best interests at heart.

Chapter 16
Bad Professors/Impossible Exams (What To Do)

Let's talk about what some may call "Bad Professors and Impossible Exams."(When I say "bad" I mean bad as in, "poor in their ability to instruct or teach," or bad simply due to their grading system, etc.)

> **If you haven't already, at some point you will most likely come across a professor who you believe is bad and gives "impossible to pass" exams.**

First of all, let me just tell you that you are not alone. Many, many college graduates, right or wrong, have believed (and some still do) that one or more of their professors were trying harder to fail them then they were to teach them. These professors are known as the kind that several students on campus will tell you, "Nobody ever gets higher than a C in her class" or "That professor is sexist. He only gives A's to the pretty girls."

Some may even say, "She just doesn't like me. She hates all athletes and thinks we all get to skate by without any effort. That's why she's so hard on me."

The truth of the matter is, those accusations may be true and they may be false. My question to you is, "Does it really matter?" I mean, think about it. Either way, whether they are guilty of such things or not, you still need to pass their class and preferably with an A, right? Besides, even if these professors are *not* guilty of such things, if your perception of them is that they are, then you'll behave like they are and most likely create problems with them that otherwise wouldn't exist.

So what do you do? Do you drop the class? Take a different route? Accept a D for a grade and thank God it wasn't an F? Well, if that's what you choose I certainly can't stop you. But I'd rather you find the best solution possible and focus on that instead. And don't worry. I've got more than one to offer you, so keep reading!

The Easy A

I remember attending a certain college (I'll keep it anonymous out of respect for the school) and having a professor who I felt had an unfair grading system and gave A's to beautiful girls only. (Whether true or not, it was how I felt at the time.) He was teaching a class that I'm sure had a purpose for being a part of my required courses but at the time I didn't think so.

SIDE NOTE: Have you ever asked these questions?

- WHY do I have to learn *this* stuff?
- WHY am I in *this* class?
- WHEN will I EVER use *this*???

Well, that was me!

Anyway, here I am in my late teens, trying to grasp the concept of what this professor was touting, while at the same time, wondering why I was even in this class to begin with! To make matters worse, this particular professor had an interesting way of collecting grades and giving exams (and I'm being nice by stating it that way, *believe me*). One way he used to get quiz grades was by taking attendance (but not in the traditional sense, like giving you a point for each class you attend and then giving you a grade based upon the amount of points you had earned out of the amount of points possible, or the number of classes you should've attended). No ... He wasn't like that. He would wait until about halfway through a 90-minute lecture and say, "Get out a sheet of paper, write your name on it, and then pass it forward to me. You just took your first quiz."

That was it. No questions, no essays ... Just write your name on a sheet of paper and ace a quiz. I thought it was a joke. Write my name on a sheet of paper and turn it in?

Something about this didn't sound right.

I mean, sure ... It's an easy A, but what about learning and being graded fairly? This was just *too* easy. If I could get an A this easy without proving I deserve it, then so could anyone else in the class who *didn't* deserve it. I didn't like this. It bothered me.

Now before I go any further I know what many of you are thinking ... "Wilson, what's wrong with you? That's an easy A! I'd *love* to have him for a professor! That class would be a piece of cake!" Well please realize, he didn't do this every class. He did it randomly, like during week #3 and again during week #7. Therefore, you could go to EVERY class EXCEPT the two classes he gave his "quiz" and you would FAIL BOTH of them (the only two quizzes he gave that entire semester)! Whereas, I could (by luck) skip every class except those two classes and ACE THEM!

Does that sound fair now? I didn't think so.

And that was just his quizzes. You should've seen his tests.

He would lecture in each class the entire time (no class discussions … just lecture) for about four weeks straight and then give us an exam. If you asked him what was going to be on the exam, he would say, "Everything I've talked about up until now."

What? What is *that*? Talk about difficult! I remember thinking,

> **"My high school teachers didn't prepare me for this. I'm in trouble."**

To make matters worse, he listed (and I remember this very vividly) 14 topics on the board that he had discussed over the course of the last four weeks. He then proceeded to tell us that out of the 14 topics listed, he was going to choose two of them, and ONLY two of them, to be on his exam. However, he wasn't going to tell us which two he was choosing, therefore we had to study all 14 of them. THEN, he stated that for each of these two topics he chooses, our assignment would be to write an essay that contains at least six major points that define each topic.

After that (Yes, I know, this is a lot! Imagine actually taking the class!), we were to list three sub-points for each of the six points we previously listed, and these sub-points must include supporting details.

WHAT? ARE YOU KIDDING ME???

If I wanna pass this test FOR SURE, I need to be prepared to memorize 24 total points per topic x 14 topics! That's 336 things I have to know for ONE TEST! And then he's only gonna question me on two topics? WHAT? (You can imagine how I felt. Although he had every right to do this, as a teenager who had pretty much skated through high school, I had never seen anything like it and I was freaking out.)

To say the least, I was ready to give up and quit. After all these years of getting by in school, I had finally met my match. Well, at least that's how I felt. (You ever felt like a test was gonna be sooo ridiculously hard that there was no point in even studying for it? That was me. I was ready to throw in the towel. In my mind I didn't have a chance. To me, it looked like I was about to officially fail my first class. And I didn't like it.)

Who's THE MAN?

To make a long story short, *he* met *his* match! I *did* memorize those topics! I studied my butt off just to prove him wrong and show him I'm not goin' out like that! And guess what I got on that test?

An "A!" What? **Yes, I said I got *an A*!** I was lovin' it!

I actually scored so high on this exam and the ones that followed that I was exempt from taking his final exam!

I remember thinkin' to myself, "Ooooooh! What's up now?! Who's the man? WHO'S THE MAN?! I AM!" It felt sooo good, too. Like I had proven him wrong or something … as if he were hired to fail me.

(Looking back now, I realize I really just needed to grow up.)

In all reality, I don't think I proved him wrong. I think I just proved to myself that I could do this thing called "college." That I *can* complete my degree. That I *can* get that diploma. That I *can* do this. And you know what? I was *right*.

How did I do it? I'll tell you in just a moment (see "My Solution Part Two: The Impossible Exams"). But first, I gotta ask … do you trust me now? Do you believe you can do it, too? I'm tellin' you … If you'll listen to what I'm sharing with you, you can truly get through your college years successfully, complete that degree, and get that diploma.

Yes … you CAN do it!

My Solution (Part 1: Bad Professors)

When it comes to bad professors and impossible exams, the first thing you need to realize is that regardless of whether either is actually bad or impossible, *anything can be accomplished with a little effort and some work.* So with that in mind, let's start with the professors.

Option 1- Been There, Done That

If you have a professor you truly believe will be difficult (unfair grading system, poor instruction, etc.) or simply just not to your liking (hey … sometimes we just "click" better with some people more than others), one solution is to find someone who's already taken their class and passed it (preferably with a "B" or higher) and get their advice.

Perhaps there's an upperclassman on campus who could let you in on a few pointers that will help you along your way, or even advise you of which professor would be best for you and your style.

This can be very beneficial in more ways than one. Besides the information you'd gain for the course, you could also develop a great friendship with them (the upperclassman).

This friendship could be one that allows for them to show you the ropes not only with this course, but with other things (like where the best pizza in town is sold, or where to get a great parking space).

So feel free to seek out other students, even if you don't have an "impossible professor." Their worth is priceless to your college survival.

Option 2- Same Class, Different Instructor
Another option you have is to investigate your course offerings and see if the class you're scheduled to take with this professor is offered by another professor now or at another time. Although I don't necessarily like this option (I don't want you to think I'm suggesting you run from things in your life every time they get a little difficult), I do realize that this course of action may be necessary. If you can find another professor offering the same course for the same credit hours, you may want to consider signing up for their class instead. Just be sure it's conducive to your overall schedule.

If the course you want to change to is going to cause you to have to graduate a semester later or put you behind in other ways, I highly recommend you try one of my other options instead. The last thing you need to do is add more time to your graduation date!

Option 3- The Summit Meeting
A third option is to meet with any professors in which you are assigned to take their course (before the course starts if possible) and ask them questions that will help you pass their course. For instance, you could ask them what it is that they expect of you as one of their students. Ask them if they have any pet peeves when it comes to class work or if there is anything they just love for a student to do (concerning the coursework for their class) that will help increase your odds of passing their course. All professors have office hours. So be smart and professional (and respectful) and visit them during their allotted times and seek their help.

If you are diplomatic and sincere I think you'll find that most of these professors aren't the "monsters" that you or the other students have made them out to be. And if by chance one of your professors *is* a "monster" (according to you, that is), at least you now know what you're dealing with.

SIDE NOTE: After writing that last sentence, I'm reminded of something a friend of mine told me years ago. He said,

> **"You can work with anthrax if you have the right suit on."**

And he's right. As deadly as anthrax is, with the right suit on, you *can* handle it, work with it, and even *survive* it.

Now I want you to know, I am by NO MEANS suggesting that your college professors are similar to anthrax or should be likened to them in any way! (Some of my former professors are incredibly caring, loving, and are why I am where I am today.)

I just want you to realize that even the toughest situations in life, no matter how difficult they may be, if handled correctly, can be dealt with successfully.

All you need are the right tools (or "suit") to complete the task. So don't run from your "monsters" in college (or in life for that matter). Just suit up, go in, and get it done!

My Solution (Part 2: Impossible Exams)

As for the impossible exams, these can be aced, too, if you play your cards right. Remember ... I passed my "impossible professor's" exams so well that I was actually exempt from his final! So it CAN be done! Trust me.

All you need to do is follow two simple steps:
* Form an alliance
* Live and die by the syllabus.

> **Now pay close attention to this next part. This is some of the best advice I can ever give you!**

Step 1: Form An Alliance
When it comes to the class you'll be attending, find two or three other students (preferably three) who are in your class and ask them to form an alliance with you (similar to a study group, but *much* more powerful).

This alliance should be formed specifically for this class and need not serve any other purpose (which is great because this understanding will free you up to form this alliance with three people that will help you pass this class and not necessarily with three people that you wanna hang out with or date). Pick people who are SERIOUS about their grades and doing the work. However, let me warn you, if you pick the cute guy or girl you secretly have a crush on, you'll spend too much time flirting with them and it will actually cost you more than help you. Leave the dating for the weekends! You came to college to get an education, so do it! Choose the right people and CHOOSE WISELY!

Now, having said all of that, the members you choose don't all have to be geniuses, either. Just make sure they're serious about passing the class with at least a B or higher. (The alliance I formed my freshman year wouldn't accept anything lower than an A. We were VERY serious!) If you have the option, pick at least one member of the opposite sex and preferably two. (The group I formed my freshman year was perfectly balanced: 2 guys, 2 girls.) This will help because men and women approach things differently and the differences will enhance your alliance.

Once you have your alliance set, have a "meeting of the minds" to discover each member's strengths and weaknesses. In my alliance, I chose a guy by the name of Greg, a girl named Lauren, and another girl named Wendi.

The Thinker

Greg wasn't the most organized but he was very good at thinking before he spoke. He was a tremendous listener (which was good for note-taking) and was well-liked by a lot of people. His viewpoints and perceptions of others (namely our professor) were phenomenal. He made a great connection with *our* professor, which helped us tremendously when it came to understanding what he (our professor) expected of us.

The Tour Guide

Next there was Lauren. She was very well organized and kept everything scheduled like a secretary. She mapped out our study nights, what we needed to know by specific dates (according to the syllabus), and provided detailed study guides. With Lauren around, we never had to worry about forgetting about a test, missing a deadline, or not knowing what to study. She was very valuable and extremely useful. Be sure you get a "Lauren" for your alliance, *especially if you're not a good note-taker.* ☺

The Event Planner

Finally, there was Wendi. She was in charge of fun stuff. You know, things like picking our place to study for the week, providing the food/snacks/drinks and the music.

SIDE NOTE: Stick with Classical instrumental … Mozart, Beethoven, etc. The lack of lyrics will allow you to concentrate without trying to sing along and the movement of the music will keep your brain "thinking skills" sharp. Repetitious music can make you tired or sleepy after a while, so save your favorite songs that you know all the lyrics to for another time!

Wendi would also reserve us a room, make sure we had comfortable chairs, computer access, and more. Basically she did whatever needed to be done to ensure that our time together was productive and <u>uninterrupted</u>. Having a comfortable, private, studious place to study was and is VERY important! There's nothing worse than trying to have a study group in your room while your dorm suite residents are blasting music, goofing off or interrupting your group constantly. You definitely wanna get a "Wendi" for your group.

> ### *Where and how you study is every bit as important as what you study. Believe me.*

What's that?

You wanna know what my role in the alliance was?

The Author

Well what do you think it was? I was the writer, of course! I had a way of taking difficult writings and ideas and explaining them in such a way anyone could understand them. This was great for putting together our essays, projects and oral presentations. I was also used as an editor and "teacher" of my other members' work. I would "grade" anything they wrote for themselves … You know … I'd look it over and correct it or revamp it a little so that it had a certain ebb and flow to it. My role was vital to the actual product that we turned in to our professor.

Our alliance allowed us to share in the anxiety that came with our exams and the understanding of just how important it was to pass them. With four of us working together, we no longer felt alone, facing this giant we call an "exam" and hoping to win. No, that wasn't us. When the four of us came together we felt *powerful*.

I'm telling you, by the time we walked out of our first meeting we were unstoppable! That impossible professor/exam didn't seem so impossible anymore. The four of us made a great team. We completed that course with such high grades that ALL FOUR OF US WERE EXEMPT FROM OUR FINAL for having aced all our previous exams! It was sooo empowering. We had a new outlook about college and our classes. We were ready for anything the next four years would send our way.

> ### *To us, there was no such thing as an impossible exam. The only thing impossible to us was failing.*

And that can be exactly how it is for you.

Get your people and form your alliance and discover each other's power. Just don't overdo it. Get too many people involved and you'll just have more problems than solutions. Remember, you're not trying to have a party, or make new friends with this alliance. So keep it simple.

And while you're at it, why stop here? Use this alliance for other classes, too. Or, just form new ones as each semester comes along. It's just that easy.

Step 2: Live And Die By The Syllabus

> *Syllabus: an outline of what's expected of you (and when) by your professor within the course of study for that particular class.*

I don't know how else to put it. That syllabus that your professor gives you is your **life**line to every **dead**line. It will keep or kill your grade, so guard it, learn it, and live by it! At the collegiate level, excuses for why your work is late, like "I had practice last night and didn't get home 'til late" or "I had a flat tire yesterday and had to spend the entire day at the auto shop" won't work. Why? Because whether you have a good reason or not for having the required work completed on time doesn't change the fact that you knew this work would be due on this date weeks (or months) ago.

You are given a syllabus for a reason: to <u>know what is expected and when</u>.

It removes all doubt of what is required of you. So don't let it become your enemy. Instead, make it your *weapon*. Use it to your advantage.

In the alliance that I had formed, Lauren handled this type of stuff for us. She would look at our syllabus and say, "Our first exam is in four weeks, so let's pretend like it's actually in three weeks and plan accordingly. We can make up our own pretend version of the test, take it, grade it, and then see if we are prepared or where we need improvement. The good thing is, we'll still have one full week to prepare for whatever we miss."

This was <u>brilliant</u>.

We operated like this for all of our exams. (I even use this technique today for other things as well.) We became so good at it, that by the time we actually took our real exams, they seemed almost trivial. All we had to do was what we had practiced over the last month. It worked like a charm.

Remember, *how you practice is how you perform*. So practice well.

Chapter 17
How To Choose the Right Major

I'm sure you've heard someone say something like "Smoking and obesity are two of the biggest causes of preventable deaths in America." We've all heard statistics like these and although they are certainly nothing to be taken lightly, why then does it seem like so many people do? Why do people continue to do something they know is causing them harm when it *can* be prevented?

When it comes to smoking and obesity I'm sure the answers are numerous, and although these are very serious concerns within our world, they are not the focus of this book or this chapter. However, I do wanna use the issue to convey my point to you concerning choosing or changing your major.

Just as smoking and obesity are serious problems that greatly decrease the quality of a person's life (and in their worst stages, can bring about the death of the person), so are choosing the wrong major, or changing it (especially over and over again) serious problems in your college life that will decrease the quality of your overall college experience. Not knowing what career to choose or constantly changing your mind about it will add more and more time to your final graduation date, more money to your college bill, more work to your work load, more classes to be completed, and in its worst state, it too, can bring about death ... the death of your college career.

But just as smoking and obesity are considered to be problems that are preventable, so, too, are the problems of choosing the wrong major or constantly changing it.

Believe me, you don't have to wander around campus from one semester to another wondering if you made the right decision, second-guessing your career of choice, and constantly dropping one class only to enroll in another. You *can* prevent this and I'm going to show you how.

My Solution

The way to prevent choosing the wrong major or the constant changing of it is similar to the way you prevent a divorce: you pick the right one the first time and you don't have to worry about wanting another. I know, I know ... that's easier said than done, but it *can* be done. It just takes some forethought and planning. So let's do it.

Before we begin, we'll have to address your issue based upon where you are in your college career. Most likely, you fall into one of two categories when it comes to the types of people who will read this book: those who are about to go to college and those who have already started.

I'm asking you to read both sections (whether you feel they apply to you or not) because a lot of the advice I give to one group also applies to other. This way I won't have to repeat myself, and you won't miss anything. Cool? Cool.

For Those About To Rock (Go To College) ... I Salute You

In keeping with our marriage/divorce comparison mentioned earlier, when it comes to your major, picking the right one is similar to picking the right mate. Before you even start, you've gotta know what it is exactly that you want, and then ask yourself questions that will give you answers to help steer your journey. Questions like; "Is what I want reasonable? Is it something that will want me back? Is this *really* what I want, or is this what everyone's telling me I want? Do I even *know* what I want?"

Although there are many more questions I could list here, those are great ones to start with. So we will!

When I say you've gotta know what you want, what I mean is, you've gotta know what it is you wanna be once you've graduated. Do you wanna be an educator? Doctor? Writer? Politician? Lawyer? Athlete? Trainer? Business executive? Advertiser? Dietician?

What is it *you* wanna be?

The possibilities are endless, but the colleges that offer these aren't.

Some have exactly what you're looking for, others don't. So rather than picking the college with the best parties, the one closest to home, or the one that "everyone is going to," *pick what it is you want to do first*, (you know, figure out exactly what it is you wanna be when you grow up) and *then* find all the colleges that offer you a degree in that field.

You don't wanna get this backwards. Trust me.

The Dating Game
I've seen people pick someone to date or marry based upon simple, shallow ideals. Anything from choosing a mate because they thought they were cute to choosing them because their parents liked them. This would be like you choosing a college because you think it's cool or because it's where your parents or siblings went to school. Although both of those reasons are welcomed (and can certainly play a role in your decision-making process), they're not deep enough to build your future career and livelihood upon. You'll need more than this to build your foundation. (Not only in a college, but in a mate as well!)

So choose your school for more than cosmetics and emotions. *Choose the one that's for you.* Don't be like sooo many who have come before you and floundered or failed. Learn from their mistakes. Learn from *mine*. It will save you from feeling stuck in a school you don't like, with a major you never really wanted, and a career choice you've never felt certain about.

Oh yeah … One other thing I almost forgot to mention:

DON'T CHOOSE YOUR MAJOR OR YOUR COLLEGE JUST BECAUSE IT'S WHAT YOUR BOYFRIEND OR GIRLFRIEND IS DOING OR WHERE THEY'RE GOING!

Let me tell you … 99% of the time this is a really bad idea! Now please note, I didn't say it's a bad idea to go to school where your boyfriend or girlfriend attends, I simply said that he or she should not be the reason you choose your major or your college. If you "do the math" and everything looks like the best choice for you happens to be where your girl or guy is attending, then great! More power to ya! Just know that oftentimes students choose their school based solely on the idea that it is where their boyfriend or girlfriend is attending, and quickly find themselves in a relationship that didn't last and now second-guessing their choice of college (not to mention having to see their ex all over campus). It's just not a good idea.

Going … Going … Gone!
Years ago, Bobby, a friend of mine, and I were working out at the local gym. We were in the middle of one of our sets when in walks this girl that was sooo attractive practically every guy in the place stopped what they were doing just to watch her walk by. As she passed us and entered the girls' locker room, Bobby looked at me and said, "What was *that*? That girl is absolutely beautiful! I'm going to ask her out."

I remember thinking, "He doesn't have a chance with her. She won't even give him the time of day. This oughta be interesting."

Well, he did ask her out, and to my surprise, she accepted. Even crazier, within two weeks, they were, as he put it, "a committed couple." I was shocked, but

95

happy for Bobby. That is, until he told me the rest of his "good news." He went on to inform me that he was transferring from his current school (where he had just completed two years of a four-year program) to West Virginia University (WVU). I asked him what prompted him to want to transfer to WVU. He had never mentioned going there before, and although I felt it was a great school (several of my high school buddies were attending there and I had visited the campus many times), I didn't understand Bobby's sudden interest.

Do you wanna take a wild guess as to why he decided to change schools right in the middle of his college experience?

(I know, I know … the suspense is killing you, right? *Yeah right*. I think we all know exactly why Bobby changed schools.)

Bobby changed schools so he could go to school where his new girlfriend was already attending.

And what do you think happened only a few weeks after he arrived on campus?

Wait for it … Wait for it …

BAM! His new girlfriend broke up with him and started dating someone else!

(Did you see that coming, too? Because Bobby didn't! He was devastated.)

Not only had he lost his girl to another guy, he was now on a campus where his new ex-girlfriend was also, so not only is he now suffering from depression and lovesickness, but he also has to take the chance of running into her (and possibly her new boyfriend) all over campus. To make matters worse, some of his courses taken from his old school had not transferred to WVU (which only added time to his graduation date) and now, after just moving everything and getting things set up, he was seriously contemplating transferring back to his old school.

In the end, his girl left him, he left her school, and one year later he ended up right back where he started from (back at his old school). Only now he had managed to add an additional year to his graduation date as well as spend more money on classes he never completed, travel he could've avoided, and other expenses that were basically for nothin' (not to mention his broken heart).

SIDE NOTE: *Anything you can gain quickly in life you can usually lose quickly as well*. Like the way Bobby quickly became committed to his girl in just two weeks, only to lose her within a few weeks afterwards. On the other hand, anything that takes a while to gain tends to be harder to lose. Just remember,

> ### *Oak trees don't grow overnight, but weeds do.*

(Yep … like sooo many others, I want you to read that one again.)

So learn from Bobby's mistakes. Be sure to choose *your* school and major because they're what's best for *you*. Not your boyfriend or girlfriend, not your parents, not your high school buddies, but for you. If you don't, you are seriously risking your chances of survival. At best, you'll add more work to your load, graduate later than planned, and add more debt to your life. At worst, you'll drop out, not graduate at all, and *still* add debt to your life.

And what does all of this school choosing have to do with preventing you from changing your major? Well, if you choose the wrong school (one that doesn't offer your major or one that offers you something close in your field but not quite what you need) you'll end up not only wanting to change your major, but your school as well. College students do this *all the time*. And besides all the problems it adds to their college experience (time, money, energy, etc.) it also leaves a negative impression on them about college and their future with it.

Breaking Up Is Hard To Do
Just like many hurt, disgruntled lovers blame the break-up on the other person involved in their relationship, so, too, do these college students blame their "break-up" with their school (reason for transferring or dropping out) on the college. And unfortunately, it's usually the student's fault and not the school's.

Now I realize that this is something you may not wanna hear. Believe me, **I know schools have their problems**. Really I do. **But for the most part, poor reasoning for students transferring isn't one of them**. Students know (or should know and certainly *can* know) what they're getting into *long before* they sign the dotted line. The majors offered by the schools they're attending were all listed in the school catalog back before they ever applied. All they had to do was read.

And while I'm at this, please don't think I'm reprimanding or preaching to you for changing your major (or anyone else that has).

Don't forget, I changed my major, too (*and* transferred, *and* dropped out, before finally going back and finishing).

Research shows that college students often change their majors two or three times (or more) during their college career. So believe me, this is nothing new. But just because "everybody's doing it" or has already done it, it doesn't mean *you* have to. There are ways to prevent this from happening and I've included them in this section for you (see "5 Steps To Help You Choose Your Major").

Taking the steps I've listed will greatly increase your chances of picking the right school for you and your major long before you ever commit to one.

This school will be THEE school for you ... the school you'll love ... the school that will love *you* ... the school you'll be proud to say you not only attended, but *graduated* from. And why? Because knowing what you want to be in life will steer you in the direction of the right major, which in turn, will steer you to the right school.

This will greatly enhance your chances of not only sticking to your major (instead of changing it two or three times), but also sticking to your school and eliminating transferring or dropping out as well. A decision like this will affect you the rest of your life (financially, culturally, socially, etc.).

Don't settle.

Don't follow the crowd.

Don't do it for anyone else but you.

It's your career and your life. Make it *your* choice.

P.S. If by chance you're reading this and thinking, "That's great advice and all, but **I have no idea what I want to be when I grow up** (what to declare as my major). How in the world can I make all these choices when I can't even figure out what I wanna be?"

If this is you, then I have a question for you: **How can you possibly pick the school that's perfect for you when you don't even know what it is you want to be?**

> *I'm amazed at how many students can tell me in their early high school years what college they wanna go to but they can't tell me what they wanna be when they grow up!*

Instead of picking their major (profession, career, etc.) first and then finding several schools to choose from that offer such degrees (and scholarships for some talent they possess), they pick the school they wanna attend FIRST and then ask the school what degrees they offer!

WHAT? (Does anyone else see the problem with this besides me?)

LISTEN TO ME. Before you pick your school, you *really* should pick your major. Get these backwards and you're greatly increasing your chances of changing majors *and* schools. And that's not good.

Ever Heard Of A Personality Test?
If you need help picking a major, or choosing a career, there are tools available to you (many at no cost) that will help steer you in the right direction.

For example, the *Minnesota Multiphasic Personality Inventory* (more commonly known as the MMPI or "personality test") is a popular test that has been used for years to identify not only psychopathology (google it if you want), but also personality traits in people for general purposes (employment positions, background checks, etc.). A test like this can tell a possible employer, doctor, or even the test-taker, a lot about who they are (the test-taker, that is), what they like or don't like, and what they would most likely be best suited for in a line of work (career, employment positions, and more).

Although the MMPI wasn't exactly designed for future college students to decide their major or career, there are several tests that are, or at least can help steer you in the right direction (like the *Myers-Briggs Type Indicator* or MBTI). Many of these tests are designed specifically to help you choose a career, or simply tell you more about yourself. (I wish I had known about these when I was in your position. You are sooo lucky!)

These tests are often referred to as career aptitude tests, career interest surveys, career choice tests, interest assessments, self assessments and many, many other names (too many to list here).

Most of these tests can be found online, but your school (high school or college) will most likely have an official version of one or more of these for you to take, as well as a trained and licensed person (guidance counselor, advisor, etc.) to implement it for you! In most cases, all you have to do is ask! (Isn't that nice?)

So if you're finding it difficult to pick your major/career, I strongly suggest you take a personality test, as well as adhering closely to the following guidelines I've listed below. They will benefit you greatly, and save you a lot of time, money and energy.

---

5 Steps To Help You Choose Your Major

Step 1: Decide what you wanna be "when you grow up" *first*.

Step 2: Make a list of all the colleges you like that offer a degree in the career you've now chosen.

Step 3: Narrow the new list you've now created down to only the colleges that offer scholarships.

Step 4: Investigate the schools you now have remaining on your list.

Step 5: Schedule a visit to each of the final 3-5 schools left on your list.

Step 1: Decide what you wanna be "when you grow up" _first_. Contact your high school guidance counselor or your college advisor, tell them you're interested in taking a career aptitude test (or something similar), and begin the process of finding out what career would be best for you.

Pick a major that will put you into *that* career.

Pick a college that offers *that* major.

Step 2: Make a list of all the colleges you like that offer a degree in the career you've now chosen (and preferably colleges within a two-hour driving distance or less. This makes transportation and all matters related to it much easier).

Step 3: Narrow the new list you've now created down to only the colleges that offer scholarships for a skill or talent you have (I discuss why this really matters in much more detail in the "My Solution" section of Chapter 29).

Step 4: Investigate the schools you now have remaining on your list (go to their websites, get some brochures, free materials, etc.) and learn more about them. What do you like or dislike about them? Are they in a good location? Are they progressing? What's their campus culture like? (See *Campus Personality aka "Campus Culture"* listed in Chapter 1 for more on Campus Culture.) Once you've investigated these schools, you should find that there are some that really appeal to you and others that don't at all. Therefore, you are now ready to narrow your list again. Do your best to narrow it down to roughly 3-5 colleges.

Step 5: Schedule a visit to each of the final 3-5 schools left on your list. Be sure to take a parent or guardian and at least one person you know who has already graduated from college (they'll know what to look for, who you'll wanna talk to, and what questions to ask once you're on campus).

That's it! Follow those guidelines and you are well on your way to successful, *happy* college career!

(And <u>YES</u>, I DO know that visiting up to five schools can be time consuming. If you spent two days at each one that would be 10 days of your life. Yes ... I realize that. But if I would've spent 10 days of my life doing this when I was in your position I wouldn't have spent **six years** in college spread out over **eight years** of my life just to get a **four-year** degree! Think about it.)

Now ... Before I move on to the next section (concerning those already in college), I am asking you to please read it as well, even if you haven't started college yet. *Trust me.* The information within it is still very useful and will benefit you throughout your college career. I promise!

Chapter 18
Is It Okay To Change Your Major?

Before you read this section, please be sure to read *"For Those About To Rock (Go To College) ... I Salute You"* (previous chapter) first. It has valuable knowledge in it worth reading, regardless of your current collegiate status.

Now ... Let's get started.

99 Problems And Graduation Is One (Those Already In College)
As I mentioned earlier, I will keep with our marriage/divorce comparison to help with the explanation of this section. With that in mind, if you are already in college, then you are like a lover who has already committed to someone; in other words, it's like you're married. You picked a mate (college and a major) that you liked/loved at the time (it was what you thought you wanted to be), but now for some reason, the "love" just ain't there anymore (you're hating your classes and finding out this career choice just ain't for you!) and now you wanna play the field and date others (change your major) or get a divorce and start all over (transfer or dropout).

So what do you do? What *can* you do?

Well, I'm not gonna lie, just as divorces can get messy, so can changing your major. But there's hope! With the right lawyer, you increase your chances of getting all you deserve out of what's left of your marriage. And with the right guidance (like I'm giving you in this book) you can get all you deserve out of what you've invested up to this point in your college career. It will cost you a little (there's really no getting around that) even if only your time. But I'd rather it cost you a little time now than a lot of time and frustration later. Right? Right. So follow my guidelines and you can keep your risks, expenses and frustrations to a minimum.

WARNING: I am not a genie or a psychic! I cannot see your current situation or your immediate future. Please remember this book is a survival *guide*, not a genie in a bottle. So since I do not know your exact circumstance, I cannot give you an exact answer. For any special circumstances, you may want to consult someone you trust to help guide you. However, as with any counsel, I strongly recommend that your counsel come from more than one person and that all persons giving you counsel should have your best interests in mind.

Also, please be sure that the majority of those giving you advice not only be people who have gone to college themselves, but they should also be graduates, too. If you wanna know how to stay in and graduate, it only makes sense to get advice from those who have. Now, having said all that, let's start with a basic guideline that should fit <u>most</u> of you that are dealing with the dilemma of changing majors.

My Solution

---

4 Steps To Help You Decide If You Should Change Your Major

(And how to do it with the least amount of damage to your college career)

Step 1: Be honest with yourself about your current situation.

Step 2: Get to the root of the problem.

Step 3: Decide what you wanna be when you grow up.

Step 4: Let your timeline direct your next move.

Step 1: Be Honest With Yourself About Your Current Situation. Why do you feel the need to change? Or a better question might be, "Why did you choose this major to begin with?" Did you pick it because someone at your high school told you to? Did you do it to please your parents? Did you choose it because your sister did, too? Did you simply just make a mistake? Answering these questions honestly will help you make a better decision.

Step 2: Get To The Root Of The Problem. How do you do this? Let me give you an example. If after completing Step 1 you now believe you chose your major because it's what your older sister chose when she went to college, my next question to you is "why?" Why are you doing what she did?

Are you competing with her? Following her? Perhaps just wanting to prove to her and your family that she's not the only smart one in the family?

Although I feel for you (really I do … my older brother was sooo much better in sports than I was growing up. I just wanted to be good at something. It was a lot of pressure for me), reasoning like this is not good enough to choose a major *or* change one.

It really comes back to what I've been saying all along: what is it that YOU wanna be when you grow up? If you choose your major and career for any other reason, the odds are that you may still not be happy even if you're successful in your career, simply because you run the risk of having a career that you truly don't want or simply isn't "you."

SIDE NOTE: As I'm sitting here writing this book, a good friend of mine stopped in for a visit. He slowly began reading what I had written on the screen, and in a very assertive, but genuine manner, stated the following:

> **"Why don't you tell them to stop playin' video games all day, partying every weekend, looking for a mate, or thinking they've got all the time in the world, and get real with themselves and figure out what they wanna be!"**

Now I certainly don't wanna come off rude or insensitive, especially to some of you younger readers who may only be in the early stages of high school. My friend's advice may not even apply to you. However, my concern is that for some of you, this may be *exactly* your problem. I mean, my friend *does* have a point. You gotta get real with yourself. This *is* your life we're talking about. It's *yours*, and it's the only one you get.

So please (and I say this in the most caring, cautious tone possible), get serious about who you are, what you are, and what you wanna be before you wake up 5-10 years from now with a ton of debt and no degree. Believe me, it's not a good thing to do. And the longer you wait, the more difficult it becomes.

Time goes by fast. Seriously. *And life does not wait for those who do.*

Okay, okay … I'm done being your parent. Thank you for allowing me to play that role for a brief moment. I appreciate it! Just remember, I'm on *your* side. I DO care. And I want the best for you. And I'm sure my friend does, too!

So please consider this advice and get to the root of the problem. Determine exactly *why* you chose *what* you chose as a major. If you did it for any other reason than "Because this is exactly what I want to do as a career for the remainder of my life" (or the larger portion of it) "and I truly believe I will be happy in this field" then I highly suggest you *seriously* consider changing it.

Step 3: Decide What You Wanna Be When You Grow Up. Yes, you should've done this first, I know. But remember, this section is for those of you who have already started college (or already declared a major). So before we can answer this we had to complete Step 1 and 2 first to decide if we even need to go any further in the first place. So, assuming you did complete those steps and still believe you need to change your major, let's take a look at Step 3.

If you need help deciding what you wanna be, I can tell you an easy way to find out. Take my advice I mentioned earlier (see the section labeled *"Ever Heard Of A Personality Test?"* in the previous chapter). Once you've done that, list 5-7 careers you think you'd like to have, go spend a day or two with someone already in that career and see what it's like. That will tell you better than any book or advice I can give you. And besides, it works.

I remember I used to think I wanted to be a high school principal. So one day I called up my old principal and asked him if I could shadow him for a day. He gladly obliged and one week later I was at his school. It only took one day for me to realize that what I envisioned a principal doing and what is actually expected of them are quite different. It was at that point that I decided to stay with teaching in the classroom. That visit with my principal saved me a lot of time, money, energy, and many, many days going in a direction that just wasn't for me. It worked for me. It will work for you.

Step 4: Let Your Timeline Direct Your Next Move. When I say "timeline" I'm talking about the basic time it should take you to finish your degree. It can be a real timeline or an imaginary one. Just visualize the timeline and where you are on it. For example, if you are enrolled in a basic four-year program and you are nearing the end of your sophomore year, then you would be located at the halfway point on your timeline. Make sense? Now, keeping that in mind, depending upon how close you are to graduating, you may or may not want to change your major. (For more help on this concept, I've included "The Graduation Timeline/Guideline" for you next.)

The following timeline/guideline is based upon a standard four-year degree:

The Graduation Timeline/Guideline

SENIORS   Start  Finish

If you are 75% or more finished (at least three out of four years complete), then most likely you should stay right where you are and complete your current major. You're practically finished. Why do you want to change your major now? What happened? What changed?

These are serious questions that require serious, thoughtful answers. *Changing your major this late in the game is strongly unadvised* and I would never do so without consulting at least three or four adults who know you and can truly help you make the right decision. *Can* you change your major now? Sure. Should you? I'd say there's about a 90% chance you shouldn't. So don't make any major decisions without some wise counsel first. I also highly recommend that at least three of the four adults you talk to for advice be college graduates.

JUNIORS   Start Finish

The advice I gave the seniors is basically the same advice I'm giving you as well. If you are 50% or more finished (at least 2 out of four years complete), then you are past the halfway point! Why stop now? You're on the downside! It'll go by faster than you think. However, I do know that some majors have you spend your first two years of college taking basic classes that all majors often are required to take.

It *is* possible that during your junior year you are just now entering the program that is required for your degree and are actually experiencing for the first time what it is that will be expected of you from your future career. Now that you are getting your feet wet, you may be finding this career isn't quite what you thought.

(This happens with students in the education field a lot when they actually step into a classroom and see what it's really like to be a teacher. Some students get one dose of those kids acting up and decide maybe being a teacher isn't quite for them.)

If you find yourself in this predicament and you feel you really must change your major, my advice to you is to investigate the possibility of changing to a major that is a modified version of what you're already doing. For example, if you have two years finished in the education field, I don't recommend starting

106

all over and trying your hand at a career that is so opposite of the one you've been pursuing that none of the classes you've already completed transfer. *You picked this field for a reason.* If that reason is still valid, then maybe you can stay within your major or field, but choose a different position within it. This will reduce the chances of you having to take a lot more classes and will also increase the odds of more of your completed classes transferring to your new major. (After my freshman year, I changed my major from Physical Education to Elementary Education because I wanted to stay in education, but I didn't wanna stay in the gymnasium. I wanted to teach in the classroom. Make sense?)

So basically, I recommend staying where you are, but if you must change, try to stay in the same overall field of your current major if possible.

SOPHOMORES   Start  Finish

Good news! You can probably change your major at least once this late in the game and not cause too much damage. Why? As I stated earlier, a lot of the classes you were required to take during your freshman year were most likely classes that everyone is required to take, regardless of their major. Sure, there's always an exception or two, but for the most part, changing your major before or during your sophomore year isn't quite as harmful as it can be during your junior or senior year. But please note, this doesn't mean you *should* change your major. You still need to answer the same questions as the others: Why do you wanna change your major? What happened? Is it your major that needs changed or are you just frustrated with a specific professor or class?

> ### Don't make a permanent decision during a temporary situation.

Before you go jumping ship, be sure to check with three or four trusting, college-educated adults about your situation. You may find you don't need to change your major at all. Perhaps you just need to lighten your load this semester, or drop a certain class and take it with a different instructor next semester. Whatever you do, do it with the least amount of time added to your timeline as possible. You may even want to take a class or two over the summer to make up for any possible loss of time so as to stay on schedule for your graduation date.

FRESHMEN   Start ★☆☆☆ Finish

If you are a freshman and you want to change your major, I'd say the odds are pretty good that the problem isn't that you don't like your current one, but rather, that you don't really know for sure what it is you wanna be when you grow up. Rather than jumping into another major, I recommend you at least finish your current semester and while doing so, you take a long, hard look at your future.

You may wanna go back and re-read the previous section *"Those about to start college"* and go through all of those checkpoints first. The one thing I will say is, if you're absolutely sure you must change your major, this is the best time to do it, before you get in too deep and spend valuable time, money and resources that you cannot get back. But as always, please do not make this decision on your own. Find three or four trusted, educated adults to help steer you in the right direction.

THE BEST COLLEGE STUDENT SURVIVAL GUIDE EVER WRITTEN

Chapter 19
Is It Bad To Transfer to Another School?

It happens every year: Student goes to college. Student "tries" college. Student doesn't do so well at college (socially, academically, financially, or otherwise). Student leaves college.

Scholarships are lost. Money is lost. Time is lost. Effort is lost. Patience is lost.

> ***If I had a dollar for every student who has dropped out of college or transferred to another one unexpectedly, I'd have enough money to pay off my student loans!***

I'm not kidding. This kind of thing happens *all the time*, but it doesn't have to. Many students second-guess their choice of college early into their freshman year, or sometime before the end of their sophomore year.

I've heard the all too familiar questions:
* Should I stay?
* Should I go (and come back later, or drop out altogether)?
* Should I transfer to another school?

These questions arise, but almost ALWAYS for the wrong reasons. Let me explain.

Many of us (and I really mean just about all of us) do NOT like change! We don't adapt well. We could, but we don't. Why? Because we've just spent the first 18 years of our lives (or more) building our reputation, our friendships, our comfort zones, our talents, and even our ability to like or accept who we are. We finally get this understanding in place and feel stable (for the most part) and what happens? We're whisked away to some school two or more hours away where nobody knows our name, our reputation, our skill-set, our friends. Everything we've worked so hard to build and secure to this point in our lives has just been reduced to little or nothing (or so it seems) and starting all over again just doesn't sound like an option.

Now for some of you, this is good news. You can't wait for a new beginning. But don't be fooled: even those seeking new beginnings fall prey to the "Should I stay or should I go?" experience. And for the rest of us, we're beginning to feel the pressure of that age-old question, "What if my parents were right?" We're thinking, "Maybe I should've stayed at home and gone to the community college just up the block." Or less popular ones like "What was I thinking? I hate cold weather. Why did I ever choose this place?" or "Why didn't someone tell me it was going to be this hard? Am I really ready for college?"

Whether those questions ring true for you (or others just like them), the bottom line is this: you're here now. You might as well do something with the gift and rare privilege you now have: the opportunity to get a college degree.

What Were They Thinking?

Students leave college for all the wrong reasons: loneliness, homesickness, the girlfriend or boyfriend back home, laziness, unhappy with the number of things to do or places to go in their college town, etc. The list goes on and on. But let me tell you, there really is only one *good* reason to leave college. Can you guess what it is? After reading all that I've written so far, it should be easy to figure out.

The only *good* reason to leave college is because you graduated!

This is the one and only *good* reason to leave college. Now am I saying there aren't other good reasons to leave? Reasons like "I flunked out," "I truly HATE this place," "I can't pay my bill," "I'm pregnant," etc. Well, those may be reasons you HAVE to leave (or want to leave), but are these "good" reasons? In other words, were these reasons part of your plan? Your college roadmap? Probably not. In all likelihood they're reasons that are *necessary* due to unforeseen circumstances or due to a lack of planning (or maturity) on your part to ensure that such reasons wouldn't arise.

Now I don't want that to sound mean. I really don't. I do realize that these reasons (and some similar to them) are very practical reasons to leave college. But that's just what they are ... *practical*. I want you to leave for more than a practical reason. I want you to leave for a *good* reason: because you graduated!

Girls! Parties! Fun! (Or Not)

Just so you know, I've been right where some of you are right now. During my first year of college, I had a *practical* reason for leaving college, *but not a good one*.

I was unhappy and wanted to leave after only one month! Why? Well besides feeling homesick and lovesick (remember Chapter 3?), I thought it was too boring, there weren't enough girls, and I felt like I was out in the middle of nowhere. I wasn't having the kind of fun I'd seen all those college students in the movies having and I definitely wasn't happy.

Whether true or not, this was how I felt. However, *these reasons aren't reasons to leave college. These are reasons to choose a different one before ever applying to go to college in the first place.*

"But Wilson," some of you may say, "are those reasons *really* good reasons to choose a different college? Not enough girls? Not having fun? ... Seriously?"

My answer to you is "Well kind of." You see, it's not because of the lack of girls, or the parties, or fun. No ... those are not the reasons. The real reason is because they all led back to one thing: *I was unhappy.* And let me tell you, if you're unhappy and miserable in school, it will be very hard to do well in your courses and pass, let alone graduate.

So please know, I'm NOT suggesting you choose a college based upon whether it has plenty of girls or guys to your liking, or whether they have lots of parties, or for any other petty reason.

What I'm suggesting is that you thoroughly review and study the college of your choice *before* you ever apply to it so that you are sure to choose one that you believe you will be happy to attend.

In my case, I had failed to do this.

I should've visited my college with my parents prior to attending (I didn't).

I should've stayed at my school over the weekend (prior to attending) to get a feel of student life (I didn't).

I should've talked to several of the students on campus to get an authentic response about what it's like to attend my school (I didn't).

I should've looked at the programs and courses they offer to see if my school even had what I wanted for my career (I didn't).

To make matters worse, I left after only one year and I had a scholarship that paid roughly 85% of my tuition! EIGHTY-FIVE PERCENT! Are you getting this??? I could be sitting here right now writing this book while no longer owing $60,000 in student loans! I could be debt-free of any tuition and education expenses! If I had done my research, I could've easily found out if this school was for me or not. But no … I had to be stubborn. I had to have it my way.

Instead of learning how to adapt and grow, I had to have the world stop growing and adapt to *me*. And that, my friend, is the first step to self-destruction.

If that school truly wasn't for me, I should've (and could've) known that *long before applying*. Once I was already there, I really should've stayed. I already had one year done (only three left!), I *had* made *some* friends, I *was* getting an education, and my scholarship was way too big to just walk away from.

To this day I regret leaving.

It was and still is a great school. Beautiful scenery, caring professors, and a wonderful music program. And I threw it all away because I didn't know, and refused to grow. (Sigh)

Should I have gone somewhere else in the first place? Maybe (given my immaturity). But once I had already started the four-year journey and had only three years left, I should've stayed right where I was and finished.

The Best Laid Plans Of Mice And Students …
When you transfer to another school, a lot of what you think will transfer, won't! You don't wanna be like me … Some of the classes I took at Alderson-Broaddus (A-B) to satisfy part of my required courses for their education program did not transfer to my new school, Washington State Community College (Marietta, Ohio), and I found that I'd have to take some of those same classes (or ones very similar to them) all over again! Why? Because WSCC's education program was slightly different than A-B's education program; therefore, some of my courses taken at A-B did not transfer to WSCC.

I was NOT happy.

That meant more work, more debt, and more time.

It meant I would be graduating even later than I had originally planned. **I'm telling you … I should've stayed at A-B once I was already there.**

And to make matters worse, all of this could've been avoided!

But make no mistake about it … This was *my* fault, not A-B's or WSCC's!

And just so you don't think you've got me beat, I did it again! (Can you believe it?) I transferred a THIRD time! (Talk about needing a College Roadmap bad! Oh how I wish I had a book like this back then!) This time I went from WSCC to Ohio Valley University (Parkersburg, WV) and added even MORE time to my graduation!

Whose fault was this? A-B's? WSCC's? OVU's?

Nope. It was mine. *All* mine.

About the only thing worse than me transferring all over the place and adding on more debt and more time to my graduation, is you reading this, having the chance to learn from my mistakes and yet duplicating them instead.

Pick one school. Stay in it. Graduate.

My Solution

If you're at a school right now that you're not that crazy about and you feel you must transfer or leave, that's up to you. But unless it's a very serious situation that requires you to leave, I HIGHLY recommend that you stay right where you are and finish. Besides, is it really *that* bad?

Let me ask you … Why do you want to leave?

If your answers are things like, I'm lonely, I'm tired, I don't know anybody here, there aren't enough cute guys/girls here, I'm bored, it's too hard, I wanna go back to my old job, people back home need me, etc., then I want you to consider this: You didn't go to college for the opposite of these reasons, so don't leave it *for* these reasons.

What I mean is, you didn't go to college to cure your loneliness, so don't leave it because it's not. You didn't go to college to meet a cute guy/girl (although with some of you I wonder!), so don't leave college because you haven't. You didn't go to college because you thought it would be easy, so don't leave when you feel like it's hard. **You went to college to get an education and degree, so leave it after you've been educated and have your degree!**

I realize that may sound a bit harsh and lacking in compassion for your situation, but you just don't know how much harder life will be later because of the poor decisions you make now. Trust me.

Chapter 20
How Important Are Your Grades?

I'm sure some of you may be asking, "Wilson, what about my grades? My G.P.A.? You talk about all of these other things in this guide ... hazing, forming alliances, and even impossible exams ... But what about actual grades? Or my Grade-Point Average? Isn't that important, too? How can I survive my college experience if I don't pass my classes?"

These are all great questions. When I first went to college, that was something we were told to focus on a lot. However, after completing my thesis during my master's degree program, one thing I learned was oftentimes, more than academics, it's the non-academic obstacles in life that cause the big problems that affect students' chances of graduating.

Give me a student who is lacking academically but is focused and hard-working and I'll show you a student who will graduate.

> *Show me an A+ student academically who is surrounded by all the wrong people, ideas and obstacles in life and I'll show you an A+ dropout.*

It's not that grades don't matter. Obviously they do. But until you get these other courses I've listed under control and able to be "passed," the academic side of this equation is almost pointless.

What good is it if you are a genius in math with a full-ride scholarship, yet drop out before the end of your sophomore year? Or have an incredible IQ and an amazing athletic skill, yet change your major over and over again, only to eventually drop out to accept a job before graduating?

My Solution

For now, focus on passing the courses I've listed in this book. I believe you will see that once you have these courses under control, the academic side of college is a lot more approachable and much less intimidating. If you want help with your classes or grades, form your alliances, get your Super Friends, and take the advice I've given in this book (especially in chapter 16). Your alliances, above all else, will really give you an academic edge you wouldn't have otherwise.

If you still want or need more help academically, please know that most colleges offer tutoring and other classes that will actually help you to learn how to study. (I know because I took one while I was at Alderson-Broaddus. It was very helpful!) Check with your school's administration or the advisor assigned to you for more information, and enroll in one of these types of programs. They'll teach you anything from how to take notes to learning how to speed-read. Very, *very* useful.

Chapter 21

The Freshman 15
(Are You Gaining Weight?)

Do freshmen really gain 15 extra pounds? According to research, it's more like a range from 5-10lbs. However, some gain quite a lot and the extra weight can and often does begin to affect their overall college performance. So let's take a look.

Gaining weight during your freshman year is very common and easy to do. Why? Because unless you are attending college on some type of athletic scholarship, the odds are pretty good that you're not playing sports while in college. Therefore, all those late-night snacks, weekend beer parties, and intermittent lunch and dinner routines will begin to catch up with you. Before you know it, the first semester is nearly done and you are a good 10 pounds heavier and well on your way to a full 20 pounds by the end of your first year.

This even goes for those of you who were athletic high school stars: many of you played sports year-round during your four years of high school, but aren't playing at all in college (either due to better competition, lack of interest, or possibly because you're the recipient of an academic scholarship that requires much more of your time).

All of these reasons will cause you to easily add on weight and add it on fast. It may not seem like that big of a deal now, but believe me, most people who add on that extra 15-20 pounds during college *never* work it back off. I'm not kidding. If you think it's easy to gain weight now, wait until you have a full-time job that has you sitting all day (like a computer programmer, etc.) and you're married with kids.

It doesn't get easier. Believe me.

And why is this a problem? I mean, what does gaining weight have to do your college survival? And how can you keep this from happening? Those are good questions. And I have good answers.

If I had the time (and patience) to place within this chapter all the research and evidence that has shown the negative effects that overeating and being overweight can place upon your body mentally, socially, emotionally and physically, this book would easily be over a thousand pages long (and then some).

Although I *am* currently a fitness instructor (see *"About The Author"* at the end of this book), I am not a dietician. However, I *have* hired a few to work with me and for me over the years to ensure that I'm doing my best to keep body and myself at the top of my game. (How do you think I got to be so handsome! Ha!) Anyway, I don't wanna get off-track here, so I'll keep this brief, but...

> **If you had any idea how food affects your mood, or what constantly eating junk food does to your ability to think and function properly, you'd think twice before you consume all those late-night snacks.**

Besides the fact that being overweight can greatly affect your day-to-day functions, it can also affect your overall health. So please don't take what I say lightly. I will spend more time in this chapter telling you how to avoid gaining an extra 15-20 pounds during your freshman or sophomore year, than I will on the dangers of it. But please know, if obesity is a serious concern for you, I strongly encourage you to seek professional help from someone who will treat you with respect and instruct you properly on how to become the size and weight you need to be.

Besides, who cares if you survive college if you can't survive life?

I don't mean that to be rude, *I mean that because I care*.

I want you to not only finish college, but to be around long, long afterwards to share your new knowledge and love for life with everyone else. So please heed my advice and take care of yourself. Remember, I'm on *your* side.

(I know, I know ... I got all "fatherly" again, didn't I? Sorry. It's only because you matter to me and I want sooo badly for you to succeed. But we can move on.)

My Solution

Keeping that Freshman 15 from piling on is not as difficult as you may think. It's not so much about what you eat (at least not at this stage in your life), but rather, it's about time and activity. What I mean is, when you were in high school you most likely spent a certain amount of time playing a sport, or staying physically active, or even just the fact that you could only eat at certain times of the day (like during school lunch, or when you got home from school). The problem now is that you can eat just about any time you want (sometimes even in your actual college classes) and your time isn't scheduled or regimented like it used to be.

What Time Is Lunch?

You may have a class at 8 a.m. on Mondays and Wednesdays but you might not have any classes on Tuesdays and Thursdays at all, which means you can sleep in quite late. Your eating habits will change and so will your weight.

If you like what you weighed while in high school, do your best to keep the same eating habits and schedule. If that's not enough, throw in an cardio style class on campus or at the local gym. These days there are all kinds of fun ways to lose weight. And don't do it alone, take a friend or two. You could even form an alliance (like I suggested you do for your exams) or find a Super Friend or two and stick to an accountable group with a schedule and workout routine. I did this my freshman year and it worked out quite well.

If you remember, I found one of the biggest, strongest guys on campus (Brian) and made him one of my Super Friends (see Chapter 9). He had a ton of weights and equipment in an extra suite on campus that he used to do private workouts. I asked him for some advice and help with my workouts and before you knew it, I had my own key to his workout suite! It was great. I now had a "tag-team partner" to help me stay motivated and in shape (and he did, too). It was a great friendship that still exists today.

SIDE NOTE: I had a friend of mine ask his trainer once, "What's the best physical activity for me to do if I wanna lose weight?" To which his trainer replied, "The one that you enjoy."

I gotta tell you … that's great advice. If you enjoy an activity, then it won't seem like work to you. Not everyone likes working out, or going to the gym. (Some of us, if we're honest, can be a little lazy.) But we all like something. What is it for you? Biking? Jogging? Racquetball? Hiking? Dancing? Whatever it is, do it and stay consistent. This weekly activity will be a tremendous help to burning extra calories and keeping off that weight!

And while I'm at it, don't underestimate the power of walking. Yes, I said *walking*. You'd be surprised what a brisk walk will do, not only for your body, but your mind!

So whether you form an alliance, find a Super Friend, join a gym class (or even start walking), my point is, there are all kinds of ways to keep from gaining the extra weight. The key is to expect it and prepare for it.

The 75/25 Rule

You can always do what I do now (and wish I would've thought of then) ... I live by a 75/25 rule. Basically, this means that 75% of the time (or for me, Monday through Friday) I eat healthy and "right" (plenty of fruits and vegetables!) Then 25% of the time (Saturday and Sunday) I eat whatever I want (within reason, of course). I have found this to be very helpful. Besides, since you're in college, it's more likely that you'll be tempted or offered to eat "wrong" on the weekends. So if you stick to this rule, you should do well.

(And yes, I realize those percentages aren't exact with a M-F schedule, but I think you get the idea.)

Chapter 22
Are You Thinking of Dropping Out?

So you wanna leave school early for the job opportunity with all the money? Is it a technology position? An athletic position (NFL, NBA, WTA)? Working for the family business back home?

Whatever the opportunity, I gotta tell you, *I've never seen anyone leave school early without earning their degree and it be a smart move.*

I know, I know … Some of you are saying right now, "Yeah but what about "So-and-So"… you know that rapper who dropped out and didn't finish? He's a millionaire now." Or "What about that famous athlete who dropped out early? Look at her. She's wealthy. She's doing great." Or even the social network billionaires … What about them, right?

Well, you are correct, some of these people are very wealthy, that is true, but what are the odds you will actually become a professional athlete or famous entertainer or social media billionaire? I don't mean that in a rude way, either. I'm being serious. What are the odds? Do you know?

Well the research is out there (just google it and see for yourself), and there are plenty of statistics to let you know, but to save you some time I can tell you this:

You have a better chance of being struck by lightning at some point in your lifetime than you do of becoming a pro athlete, famous entertainer, or social media billionaire.[5]

---

[5] The actual percentages and odds vary from source to source (that's why I didn't quote an exact number here), but if you do the research, you'll see what I mean. When it comes to fame and fortune, unfortunately, lightning is more likely to strike the majority of us. And believe me, I don't like those odds any more than you do.

I'm not joking. Lightning ... Who woulda thought?

With that being said, I'm not saying you *can't* become a professional athlete or entertainer, or social media tycoon. And I'm not even saying that you won't. I'm just saying it's *unlikely*. (And I say that in all kindness and truth, <u>not doubt</u>. If it's your dream or goal to go pro or become an entertainer, or create the next big social media platform, who am I to stop you? By all means, follow your dream. Seriously! Just get your degree first!)

Besides, if you do make it to the big leagues, think how much better you'd be with all that money if you only had the degree to go with it!

How often have we seen people with piles of money but no education (or understanding) of how to move in this world successfully with it, let alone, spend it? How often do we read about them losing it all, filing for bankruptcy, or wasting it on foolishness? Remember ...

> ### *A degree is more than proof of grades.*
> ### *It's proof of an education.*

Listen to me ... Don't look for a reason to get out of school. *You're better than that.* Instead, remember the reason you got in it ... to get an education and degree and live a successful, *educated* life. All that fame and fortune is just a bonus!

And that's just for those of you who can beat the "lightning odds." So what about the rest of us? The *majority* of us?

Lightning Strikes

Those of us who *don't* have the chance to leave early and make millions ... Where does that leave us? I mean, why would anyone purposely leave school early without getting their degree if millions of dollars and fame and fortune are not at stake?

Well, it's no surprise. Millions or not, it's pretty simple.

Are you ready?

Can you guess what it is?

It's the same thing we've been talking about ... MONEY! Just because it may not be for millions of dollars with fame and fortune, it doesn't mean people don't get sidetracked, or that you won't either. Money is <u>still</u> one of the main reasons why juniors and seniors (and possibly sophomores) leave college before graduating. BUT ... it doesn't have to be (or in my opinion, shouldn't be).

Listen to me … I can go on and on about this, but the truth of the matter is, this book isn't about convincing you to go to college, or to even stay in it. It's about helping you *survive* it. You don't need my help to quit school. You can do that on your own. You need me to survive it! So let's focus on that.

And just so you know, I do realize that there *are* other reasons students leave school (we've discussed several of these in previous chapters) but I'm focusing on the students who are leaving on purpose, when they don't have to, and for the promise of (or the dream of) big money.

And when does this happen? Usually during or right after their junior year.

Why? Because they now have enough of an education to possibly qualify for a job that two or three years ago they didn't.

Add to it the fact that the money being offered to them is better than anything that's been offered to them before (up to this point in their lives) and it becomes a very enticing offer.

However, if you truly want your degree – if you truly want to survive college – then you've obviously gotta stay in it to finish it. Leaving without it isn't advised.

I heard someone say one time, "I'm a pretty good duck for the shape I'm in, but I'm not the duck I could've been." And that pretty well sums up what most of the college dropouts I've talked with over the years express to me in so many words.

Can you become successful without a degree? Sure. But for every person who is I can show you about a zillion more who are (successful) *because* they stayed. (Just check the research.) College graduates (overall) tend to be considered more successful in many, many categories (financially being one of them) than most non-college graduates.

Just something to think about.

My Solution

If you're so smart and educated now (and I don't mean that sarcastically, I say that with all due respect and sincerity, so allow me to repeat it and please read it with my genuine tone and caring voice) … *If you're so smart and educated now*, then think how much smarter and more educated you'll be *after* you graduate.

And besides, you'll have your degree! And that degree will be with you all of your life, whereas, that job you quit college for may not. That job may "let you go" (fire you), dissolve, have a reduction in force, shut down, get bought-out, etc. and then where will you be? I can answer that for you. You'll be without a job AND without a degree! So DON'T do it!

If you can earn a lot of money now with only having completed two or three years of school, imagine what you'll be worth *with* a degree! Think about it.

As for the rest of you ... Those of you who think it's okay to quit school now and just come back later (if you feel you need to) ... Let me tell you ...

> ### *Going back to school isn't nearly as easy as staying in it.*

You'd be surprised how much a school's policies and programs can change in a year or two. You may drop out of school needing only two more semesters' worth of classes to graduate, only to return two or three years later to find that your desired degree now requires three or four more courses you haven't completed. Now instead of only having one year left, you have managed to add on another year (or more) on top of your original final year, and have turned what would've been a four-year degree into a five- or six-year journey. So don't do it!

Stay in school. *Finish* school. Get your degree. You'll be glad you did. And so will I.

Besides, you have the rest of your life to work. College is a time-sensitive, privileged experience. Get it while you're young and while you can. The older you become, the harder it is to finish.

Chapter 23
What You Should Be Doing on the Weekends

One of the questions I hear a lot when it comes to college survival: "Is going home every weekend a bad idea?"

To which I reply in a very assertive manner, "YES!" (A loud, resounding YES by the way.)

I can't tell you enough how important and worthwhile it will be for you to stay on campus over the weekends, but I'll try.

One major benefit of staying on campus is the fact that by doing so you will slowly begin to grab a hold of your new life (as a college student, resident and citizen of your new town) as you simultaneously begin to let go of your old life (either as a high school student, former employee back home, or transfer student from another school).

Why is this important? (I can imagine some of you are thinking, "But I like my life the way it is. Why do I have to let it go and start a new one?")

Let me tell you. Whether you (we) like it or not, we're getting older every day. We're growing, changing and moving. *Your life is going to change whether you embrace the change or not.*

So prepare for it now so it doesn't catch you off-guard later. Let me give you an example:

Home Boys
Right after my high school graduation, I had friends who didn't go to college while several did. Some of the ones who didn't thought they could hold onto and maintain their current lifestyle. (You know the types … they tend to be the ones who hang around your old high school three and four years later, still trying to

124

rule the school instead of moving on and ruling something else.) What they discovered was that their lives had begun to change, too. No longer in high school, they soon found that many of their old friends weren't around every day like they used to be. Those friends had either gone to college, moved away, or gotten married. They also found they themselves were now dealing with having to work full-time to make a living.

Their lives were changing whether they embraced the change or not.

Well just as it did for these people, changes are coming for you, too. Whether you go home on the weekends or stay on campus, your life is changing. So believe me, the sooner you embrace your new life and let go of your old one, the better off you'll be.

And please realize, I'm not saying you totally ditch your old life or bury it. I'm just suggesting you let it go. (Or maybe I should say, allow it to let you go.)

Besides, by staying on campus over the weekends, you will increase your odds of surviving your college experience and graduating on time. Why? Because you will be more likely to go to or participate in athletic games, theater productions, and local community events, etc. By attending these activities and others, you are learning your new land ... becoming a citizen of your new town, making new friends and memories that will last a lifetime (like my sister's trip with Makoto - "You have map?") You'll become more familiar with the buildings and faces you see on campus. You'll be surrounding yourself with people who are now sharing many of the same interests as you.

All of these are benefits that will not only serve to help you stay in school, but will also increase your odds of surviving college (graduating and graduating on time).

And just so you know, there are times when I *do* believe it's okay to go home. As a matter of fact, *it's encouraged*. So don't quit on me just yet. Keep reading. I'll get to that part in a minute.

A Very Expensive Weekend

As I wrote the previous situation, I was reminded of a time during my freshman year when I decided to go home over the weekend. I lived two hours away and left after my last class early on Friday so I could get home as soon as possible. I had a huge exam on Monday morning at 8 a.m. and I needed to see a lot of people when I got home and still have time to study.

When I arrived in my hometown, several of my family and friends contacted me and invited me to go and do just about anything you can think of ... church, bars, dinner, movies, ball games, etc. I had so many offers I felt like I was famous or something! It felt sooo good to be sooo wanted! It was like I went from being a "nobody" back to being a "somebody" all over again. However, all of that came with a price.

How much studying do you think I accomplished? How many of those folks back home do you think really understood the gravity of my exam on Monday?

Trying to study (or even convince these well-meaning people that I needed to) was nearly impossible. They wanted to see me and hang out, and to be honest, so did I. Needless to say, I didn't get much studying done.

Instead of going home to visit, I could've spent the time that I used traveling home and back (four hours roundtrip) to study with my alliance on campus. All that drive time could've been study time. I could've studied on Saturday or Sunday afternoon and still gone out on Friday *and* Saturday night, having a fun weekend making lots of new memories with new friends. Instead, I spent money on gas, spent time rehashing old memories with old friends (which I'm not saying is bad, but it's not like I'd been gone for 20 years … it had only been a few months!), and I missed out on several opportunities to connect with new friends, new associations, and make new memories.

Add to that the fact that I arrived back on campus late Sunday night and you can see why I didn't have much time for studying, or sleep. Let me tell you, that weekend cost me more than just money! It cost me an exam grade, the chance at making new memories, and something my body desperately needed … rest.

(Oh how I wish I could go back … You just don't know how lucky you are right now.)

My Solution

Really wanna go home? That's fine. Do it. (I'm serious. No sarcasm this time … Just do it.) Go home and sleep in your own bed, eat your mom's cooking, watch the big game with your dad. Do all those things. Celebrate your family, your hometown, your old friends. That's fine. It's okay to do these things. It really is.

Just don't do them every weekend.

Your new world and life for the next four years or more is waiting for you on campus. The more you're there, the more you can learn, improve and build that world.

The Other "75/25 Rule"
If you really wanna go home and you can't wait until the major holiday breaks to do so, then try to live by the 75/25 rule, again. Only this one pertains to home visits instead of food.

Stay on campus three out of every four weekends (or 75% of the time), and go home one out of every four weekends (or 25% of the time). This limits your trips home to roughly once a month. That is more than enough for you to get your hometown fix. And remember, there's always online social media sites and other technological advances that you can easily use daily to help keep you in the know while away from home. Besides, once you graduate, you can go back home any time you want or even move back to your hometown and work there.

For now, you're away at college, so *be away at college*. Live in the moment. It will be gone before you know it.

Chapter 24
Why Your Dorm Room Needs Help

Walk into a freshman or sophomore dorm room, especially during the first semester of school, and you're likely to find pictures, posters and various objects (from trophies and awards to old sports jerseys and theater props) that will quickly inform you of who these people are, *were*, *what* they did, and *where* they did it.

Some students will decorate lightly, while others go to such extremes you'd think their room was a shrine to their past. These items, strategically placed throughout their room, shout their past accomplishments to anyone who stops by throughout the school year. To these students, it simply represents who they are and allows anyone who visits their room to have a sneak peek into a part of their life they might otherwise not know. Although this isn't necessarily a bad thing (I kept a picture or two of my friends and family in my dorm room), it isn't necessarily a good thing, either.

Having a few pics on the wall of your friends and family from back home is fine, but don't go over-board with the idea and create a living museum of your life. Why? Because they are constant reminders of what you *did* and who you *were* and not of what where you're *going* and who *you'll be*.

I don't wanna sound harsh (I really don't…so please hear me out), but …

> *If you truly want to survive your college experience, you need to focus on where you are and where you're headed, not where you were and what you did.*

Stuck On You

Think of it this way ... Suppose you saw a cute guy or girl on campus and you asked that person to go out on a date with you. While you're on the date, how would you feel if the cute guy constantly talked about his ex-girlfriend? Or the cute girl showed you all the pictures of her friends and family since she was a kid? What if this was all this person talked about?

At first, this would seem sort of cool. It would be nice to learn more about them and see what they were like. But what if they continued to do this on every date? It would get old fast. But not only that, at some point you would think to yourself, "Geesh ... This person really needs to move on and live in the present. This is ridiculous."

Well, it's the same with you. It's one thing to have a few pics on the wall and a few props here and there. That's fine. I did the same thing. I was proud of who I was and what I'd done. My family mattered to me as well. So of course I had a few pics of them, too. But my future dreams, goals and career also mattered. And I wanted constant reminders of where I was going more than where I had been. I had big dreams and ideas and a great future ahead of me. I wasn't about to fill all that extra space in my dorm room with anything that didn't promote them.

My Solution

Don't litter your entire room with stuff from your past. Leave space for the new friends, new pics, and the new props you will be gaining throughout your college experience.

What's your major? What do you wanna be once you graduate? Put pictures, titles, and props of *those* things around your room. Remind yourself daily of why you're there and what your goal is. This will help you reach your goal and stay focused.

Are you studying to be a lawyer? Have some pictures taken with some lawyers and place that pic on the wall. Wanna be a surgeon? Take a picture of the hospital you want to work at after you graduate and put that on your wall. Want to be a professional athlete? Place posters and props on your wall of the team you envision yourself playing for one day. (WARNING: Just remember, visualizing your goal is only the start! You <u>MUST</u> take action towards it or all you'll have is a nice poster! See it, prepare for it, then **go do it!**)

Let your bedroom back home *stay* back home. Let your dorm room become your "living" room. Let it live and become "alive" with your present and future. The more it holds pictures, props and stories of your college experience, the better your odds are of feeling "at home" when you're not, and the less likely it will be for you to want to go home when you shouldn't (or don't need to).

Chapter 25
The Problem with Your College Clothing

I've never understood why anyone would attend "X University" but constantly wear t-shirts, sweatshirts, and other clothing that promotes "Y University" (especially if X University is giving them a scholarship). Why would you ever want to promote your own school's competitor? Why (some would say) would you want to "spit in the face" of your current school? Where exactly does your loyalty lie?

Now don't get me wrong, I'm not saying if you wear an article of clothing that represents another school that you are somehow a traitor or an instigator or loyal to another institution. However, maybe your clothing is (or implies that you are). Remember, *perception is everything*. When it comes to others, it's not about what you say or do as much as it's about what they *perceive* concerning what you say or do. If you say you love X University but your shirt promotes Y University, your message is confusing. It's confusing not only to those around you (family, friends, fellow students, administrators, professors) but to you as well.

A Bit Much ...
Now I realize that this may sound a bit extreme in thinking. I can hear some of you right now ... "Wilson ... I like you and all, and I think you've got some great nuggets of wisdom, but this is a bit much, don't ya think? I mean ... It's just clothing."

And my reply to you would be, "Yes, you're right. It IS just clothing and it IS a bit much. But that's the difference between *attending* a college and graduating from one: *a bit much*."

It's that little extra. That little extra that turns that 2.9 G.P.A. into a 3.0 (or higher). That little extra that gets you just enough votes when you run for student government president or some rank in your sorority/fraternity. That little extra that causes those two professors (the trustworthy ones you chose to guide you through this experience) to like you just a little bit more than the last apprentice they had.

It's always about "that little extra." It's always about being "a bit much." And that's what will separate you from the rest of your competition.

So why stop now? Why not go all the way with all that you do? Why not show your support for the institution that's supporting you? The professors that are supporting you? Your parents? Others?

I mean, think of it this way … Imagine how YOU'D feel if you were president of University O's student body government, and you hired me to come and address your school and I arrived at your event wearing University P's ball-cap?

What would you think of me? What does that say about me?

When you do the same thing, what does that say about you? Think about it.

> **When you support other schools with your clothing, etc., you're not supporting yours. It's just that simple.**

SIDE NOTE: Not satisfied with my reasoning? Don't like where this is going? That's okay. I had a feeling you may not. Just so you know, there *are* times when I believe it IS okay to wear the other school's clothing, and I don't mean for the purpose of making fun of them, either. Wanna know when? I tell you in the *My Solution* section coming up next.

My Solution

As I stated in the previous paragraph, I believe there *are* times that it's okay to wear another school's clothing, etc. So here it is: when you're not on your own campus, or when you *are* on theirs. You may say, "But Wilson, isn't that being hypocritical? Kind of two-faced?" Well, I can see why you might think that, but let me explain.

When In Rome …
Some of you may have a brother or sister who attend another school. Maybe your best friend or cousin goes to another school. Showing support of their schools when you're with them is also showing support of them. It's sort of like giving them your stamp of approval for their decision to go to college. Besides, I didn't say you HAVE to do this, I'm just offering a time when I believe it's okay for you to.

The Extended Family

There are other times to wear another school's clothing as well. For instance, you may want to wear/support other schools with your outward apparel when you are in some type of partnership with them. This is a little more rare (schools tend to hook up with businesses, not other schools), but sometimes one school is sort of a "little sister" school to another. These schools will often have programs in which you are invited to enroll in their classes for your first two years of college and then transfer to their "big sister" school for your final two years.

In cases like this, I feel it is okay to wear clothing, etc. that supports the sister school because they're sort of seen as family. But that's just about it. Any other time and you have just become a walking billboard for another school.

Wearing another school's clothing while attending yours is like saying, "Yeah, I attend University Q, but if I had my wish, I'd be at University R." Don't let this be the perception people have of you, true or not. It may not hurt you to wear another school's clothing (notice I said *may not*), but I don't ever believe it will help you. Remember, you wanna survive. Why make it harder than it has to be?

Oh, one other thing … Some of you have said to me, "Wilson, I understand what you're saying, and I agree for the most part. But what if I DO want to go to J College and I'm STUCK at K College right now? As a matter-of-fact, I HATE K College and I wish I'd never applied to be here! I should've applied at J College! What do I do?"

Well, that's simple. You don't wear either. Nobody said you HAVE to wear any clothing that supports your school or anyone else's. However, if I were you, I'd at least have ONE shirt or hat that supported the current school you're attending (like it or not) because you'll give a perception that you do support it and will most likely be accepted a little more warmly on campus by others. Now that's just my opinion, but keep in mind, I'm sharing with you all the things I wish someone would've shared with me when I was in college.

Remember, I'm on YOUR side. I have YOUR best interests in mind. Ten years from now I don't just want you to be able to say, "I attended college." I want you to be able to say, "I graduated from one."

Chapter 26
The "Stagnation after Graduation" Problem

Here's a little something extra to add to the clothing advice I've given you that I think you'll find quite interesting. I gotta tell you though, I contemplated for quite some time on whether I should even include this situation in this book (as you'll see, this situation typically occurs a little later in life ... mid to late twenties, and usually not during your college experience).

However, after much thought, I decided to include it. Why? Because I don't want you to successfully navigate through your college experience with the help of this book, only to become stagnant soon after, reflecting the typical life and style of sooo many others, (whether graduates or not), that seem to get stuck in a lifelong rut so easily. (Remember, in the business world, if two of you are the same, one of you is not necessary!)

So enjoy this one. Consider it a "freebie" for being such a good student! (And while you read it, see if you can think of anyone you know personally who fits the description I'm about to present. Hopefully, it won't describe you!)

High School Daze
Have you ever seen someone who seems stuck in a certain era based upon the clothes they are wearing? I can't begin to tell you how many times I've seen men in their 30's and 40's still wearing the same hairstyle and clothing they wore when they were in high school. Or the women I've noticed still stuck in the same outfits that were popular when they were (which is also usually during their high school days).

Why is this? Why don't they keep up with the times?

Or perhaps a better question would be "Why don't they let go of *that* time?"

I have a theory on this ...

I believe these people (and many others just like them) are subconsciously holding onto a time period in their lives when they felt the most successful. A time when they were at their peak in popularity, sexiness, and living free. This tends to be (for most people) somewhere between their junior and senior year of high school because this is usually the time when they were the most popular, had the lowest number of responsibilities (usually no bills, no kids, no debt, etc.), and received the most acknowledgments for their work (awards, trophies, etc.).

Add to that the possibility that they may have been the high school quarterback, the head cheerleader, the band soloist, or the class president and their confidence during this time will soar! Then what happens?

They graduate.

And whether they move on or not, life does (including the music, the clothing, the hairstyles, and even their friends). Eventually they wake up years later and realize they're not what they used to be and typically revert to a time when they felt best about *who* they were, *what* they were, and *where* they were.

In other words, they revert to their old hairstyles, old clothing, old music, etc. Unfortunately, they cling to such trends, styles and ideals so strongly that they have a hard time accepting anything new.

Is this a bad thing?

My Solution

When it comes to the people I'm referring to in this scenario (and hopefully *never* you!), just think of it this way: If they're holding onto the past, how can they possibly be greeting the present while reaching for the future? (People like this tend to be close-minded towards new ideas, new ways of thinking, and new … well … anything!)

Does that mean they should ditch all they know and love and become something new? Totally start all over, creating a new life, new friends, new everything?

No.

It just means that they (and you!) need to stop identifying yourself with one moment in time and realize your whole life **_IS_** the moment in time! Learn from your past, live in your present, and prepare for your future.

> ### *You don't have to forget your past, but you might need to let go of it. (Or at least loosen your grip!)*

Don't get stuck.

Time keeps moving. Music keeps moving. Clothing keeps moving.

Maybe you should, too.

Chapter 27
Great Stuff You're Missing on Your Own Campus

Skull Session

I recently visited The Ohio State University (OSU) located just miles from my home. While I was there, I had the opportunity to attend one of their pep rallies known as Skull Session. It was a Saturday afternoon and my friends and I were told great things about this pep rally, so we just had to see the show.

Now when I say "show," I mean SHOW! This pep rally had nearly 10,000 people in attendance! Yes, I said TEN THOUSAND … with thousands more denied entrance inside due to limited space.

> **With a packed house, this event had the kind of anticipation that can only be likened to a WWE wrestler making his entrance at Wrestlemania.**

OSU's marching band entered playing its theme song while thousands of fans leaped to their feet and went nuts, cheering right along. (And this was just the band. The football players didn't enter until later!) *It was overwhelming.* Like some type of pre-battle scene out of Star Wars or something. Really, really impressive. This event was well organized, very energetic (you could just feel the excitement in the air), and quite fascinating to say the least.

I remember thinking how cool (and lucky) I was to be witnessing this event. Surely they don't do this all the time. The pageantry … the showmanship. However, I was wrong. This wasn't a one-time event or even a special occasion they hold annually. As it turns out, OSU holds this type of pep rally for *every* home football game. It's a major tradition for them.

And it's really something to see.

And that's what's so sad about it …

Do you realize how many current OSU students I have met since my friends and I attended that event who have never seen/attended a Skull Session?

Even worse, do you realize how many *didn't even know it existed?*

What? This is OSU. This is "THEE" Ohio State University! How could this be?

How in the world could these students attend a school so rich and deep in tradition with such huge followings and programs and not even know about a major tradition like Skull Session? What was the problem? Why didn't they know about it? Where do they go when all of this is going on? What are they doing? And why don't they attend?

You wanna know what they told me? You wanna take a wild guess?

(I'll give you a hint: It's what practically every student I've mentioned earlier in this book did or does who has trouble surviving college.)

They told me *they go home every weekend.*

Yep. That's it. They said they go home. (I couldn't believe it either.)

Now granted, *every* student who's not attending Skull Session isn't going home *every* weekend. Some work. Some have campus jobs on game day. Some have other commitments. OSU is *huge* (in student population and campus size). Many of the school's students are from other states or even other countries. Obviously they can't *all* go home every weekend, nor do they. However, the ones I had spoken to (mostly my friends or former students of mine) *were* going home, practically *every* weekend. And many of them who weren't were still unaware of Skull Session and all that comes with it.

One of them even said, "I had no idea they even did this kind of stuff at my school."

Unbelievable.

And sad, too. These are good people. Some of them are very close friends of mine. Smart. Intelligent. Yet they had no idea about this wonderful (and very impressive) tradition. OSU (and many, *many* schools just like it) work very hard to preserve and promote their history and traditions. Not knowing about Skull Session or any other major on-campus tradition is certainly not the fault of OSU or any other school. (I've never attended OSU as a student and I'm *well* aware of it.)

And just so I'm clear, **YOU not knowing YOUR school's traditions and activities is not the fault of your school!** *You've got to get involved.* Be aware of your surroundings. Embrace your campus. Not knowing what's going on all around you could be detrimental to your survival.

And Your Point?

So what does this tell us? What can we learn from this? The more I thought about the Skull Session situation, the more I began to think … How many students have attended not only OSU, but other great schools steeped in tradition or known for having major campus activities, yet never really *knew* their school? How many of them never truly embraced their school's past or present while creating an even better future for it? How many became frustrated, bored or lonely, slowly beginning to resent attending the very school that was there to educate them … only to drop out, transfer, or second-guess choosing their school in the first place? And why?

Simply because they didn't know what they were missing, or didn't get involved in a deeper way that would be sure to cement their survival there.

So that leads me to another question …

What about you? *Your* school … *your* traditions?

What are <u>you</u> missing?

And what about other schools and other traditions?

Check out the *Notable College Traditions* I've listed next and see for yourself. You could be missing a lot more than you think!

Notable College Traditions[6]

- Boston University (*Marathon Monday*)
- Princeton (*Fitzrandolph Gates*)
- Duke (*Cameron Crazies*)
- Seattle University (*QuadStock*)
- Florida State (*Downtown GetDown*)
- South Dakota State (*Hobo Day*)
- Harvard (*Housing Day*)
- Stanford (*Full Moon on the Quad*)
- Auburn University (*War Eagle*)
- Texas A&M (*the 12th Man*)
- Howard University (*ResFest*)

---

[6] "Take Me Home, Country Roads" at West Virginia University, the Grove at Ole Miss, and Halloween at Ohio University were not listed here, due to being mentioned previously in Chapter 1.

- UCLA (*Midnight Yell*)
- Indiana University (*Little 500*)
- Mizzou (*Tap Day*)
- LSU (*March Down the Hill*)
- University of Nebraska (*Tunnel Walk*)
- Michigan (*The Big House*)
- UNLV (*Premier UNLV*)
- New Mexico State (*The "A"*)
- USC (*Save Tommy Night*)
- Ohio State (*Dotting the "i"*)
- Yale (*Spring Fling*)
- Oregon (*Pit Crew*)
- Your school? (*Your Tradition?*)

Imagine attending one of these schools without even knowing about their traditions and campus activities, let alone about a zillion other things offered on campus – things that could help you stay focused, improve your grades, graduate sooner, earn a scholarship, etc. It makes me wonder what else you (and other students) may be missing.

Do you see how this (not knowing what's going on on *your* campus or being involved with it) can affect a student's ability, *your* ability, to survive college?

> *The less you have invested in your school (time, memories, activities, friends, traditions) the easier it is for you to feel like it's a good school, but not <u>your</u> school.*

And if it's not *your* school, then why stay? This type of independence increases your odds of transferring to another school (which adds time to your graduation date) or dropping out, which is even worse!

My Solution

If you wanna graduate and graduate on time, then you've got to investigate your campus! **Learn the traditions, the songs, the programs, the scholarship opportunities, the alumni members, the "world" of your campus.** Explore it. Learn its character. It will only serve to make you more dedicated to it and thus increase your chances of graduating from it. (Research indicates that students who immerse themselves in school activities have a far better chance of graduating.)

Remember, anyone can attend college. That's easy. You wanna GRADUATE from one! That's different and *rare*. Besides, *it's one thing to not know. It's another thing to know and not do.*

You have this book. You have this information.

You have no excuse.

<u>Follow</u> the guidelines in this book.

<u>Get involved</u> in your school.

<u>Get your degree</u>.

Chapter 28

The Problem with College Credit Cards

Have you ever seen one of those credit card tents or tables that uses t-shirts, coffee mugs, key chains, Frisbees or other items to entice bystanders to stop by and inquire about the credit card being offered? (Some of these items are given away for free simply for asking about their card, whether you apply or not!)

Or have you ever received a pre-approved credit card application in the mail promising you instant cash?

If you have, the good news is, due to the Credit C.A.R.D. Act of 2009, many of these credit card booths (which used to be set up all around campuses, heavily targeting college students) and pre-approved credit card applications are no longer legal. At least not without some *major* restrictions and guidelines. The bad news is, they're still permitted to be presented in some venues and in some formats (hey, this is America ya know), and these credit card companies often target young people (normally of the college age) as future customers.

Can I just say it right now? Anytime you receive one of these applications in the mail, please, TEAR IT UP! Or, anytime you see one of these booths of future debt awaiting your arrival, please, RUN as fast as you can in the opposite direction!

Do you hear me? **TEAR IT UP or RUN!**

I can't tell you enough why you should avoid these quick and easy credit card applications. They are <u>very</u> dangerous and can have a major effect on your college survival. However, let me make a few things perfectly clear concerning the products and people that work for credit card companies and these application tables.

First of all, I do not, and I repeat, I do NOT think that all people working for credit card companies are bad. Most likely, these people are just doing their job like anyone else. Heck, you may even know one of them. Perhaps one of your friends works for one. Maybe you work for one of them yourself. I certainly don't want to sound judgmental or critical of any of these people or of you if such applies. This section of this book isn't about how bad or good I think these cards or people are. It's actually about the dangers of using credit cards at such a young age without a true understanding of how they can drastically affect your college survival (and life, for that matter).

So let's talk about you and your role with these offers and get the focus back where it belongs. Okay? Cool.

Now, when it comes to credit cards, just remember this:

> ### Credit cards for some people are like alcohol to an alcoholic: dangerous!

If you put a credit card in the hands of a college student with little understanding of how it works and an addiction for shopping, you may soon wind up with a shopaholic suffering from late payments, high interest rates, and monthly fees! And that's just the beginning.

Oftentimes, the fees and payments get so high that a lot of students end up applying for more credit cards because they can no longer pay for their everyday, normal expenses since they have to use such money to pay the monthly bill on their first credit card!

What's next? Minimum payments are often barely made, are usually late, and what you end up with now is a balance that is greater than the actual amount of what you ever used or purchased. (Forget surviving college, now you're just trying to survive life!) Over the long haul, you'll end up paying many, many times more than the original price of the items you purchased.

Do The Math
Let me give you an example. Let's say you get a credit card with a $1000 limit and an interest rate of 15% that increases to 20% if you're ever late on a payment. You have no balance yet, and you just *know* you're never going to miss a payment ... I mean, how high can they be, right? So whattaya do?

GO SHOPPING!

A few pairs of shoes, some new shirts, and a few meals for you and your friends. Why not? You deserve it right? Besides, you're working hard at school and need a break.

So you start spending here and there, racking up a decent bill (let's say $335) and you decide maybe you should lay off a bit. Then "life happens." Your car breaks down and needs repaired, or you get a parking ticket, or you get sick and need medication, or whatever. Now you are faced with a new expense totaling roughly $500. So you add that on to your card, and in all the commotion of "life happening" and your schooling (tests, studying, etc.) you forget to make your monthly payment. Now you're slapped with a 20% interest rate, not to mention an additional charge of roughly $14 for not paying off your entire bill that month, on top of the late fee for not making your payment on time (let's say another $15). You now have a balance[7] of $864.

Look at it this way:

```
┌─────────────────────────────────────────┐
│            Credit Card Costs             │
│                                          │
│    $335  miscellaneous expenses          │
│                                          │
│  + $500  emergency expenses              │
│                                          │
│    $835                                  │
│                                          │
│  + $14   monthly interest charged        │
│                                          │
│    $849                                  │
│                                          │
│  + $15   late fee                        │
│                                          │
│    $864                                  │
└─────────────────────────────────────────┘
```

You haven't even purchased anything extra beyond your last emergency expenses, and yet your bill now has an additional $29 added to it! (Monthly interest + late fee.) And if you only make the minimum monthly payment (roughly $22), your bill would actually be higher than it originally was even after you make your payment ($842 instead of $835)!

Here's where it gets crazy.

Do you realize if you make no other charges *ever* (which is virtually impossible with practically every student I've ever known) and you're NEVER late on your monthly minimum payments ever again (which would be roughly around $22 and decrease to $15 over time), it will take you more than 8 years to pay off your debt (approx. 101 months!) and you will have paid a total of $1656!!!

---

[7] This is based upon a credit card with the lowest, minimum monthly payment of the interest + 1% of the balance.

Yes, I said **ONE THOUSAND SIX HUNDRED and FIFTY-SIX DOLLARS!**

That's $821 *added* on to your original bill of $835!

And that's just ONE CARD!

Most people have anywhere between 3 to 5 cards.

Now do you see how this can affect your college survival?

If every time you get paid you've gotta use the money from your paycheck to pay one of these bills, it's not long before you can't afford to "exist" where you are. Before you know it, you're transferring to a closer school back home (which will add more time to your graduation date) or dropping out altogether just to work full-time so you can pay your new bills! It's a vicious cycle that normally ends with the ever-so-innocent college student finding themselves three or four years later with five or more credit cards, each maxed-out or over the limit, working full-time just to make ends meet while all along still having *no degree*.

I'm telling you, it's VERY DANGEROUS. Seriously.

In the end, these cards can cost you so much more than you ever expected, and unfortunately, some of you will never get them paid off. (Yes … I said *never*.)

My Solution

Plain and simple: Don't get them. Seriously. None of them … not even one! The way things work today, just about anyone with a bank account can get access to just about anything they need via the Internet or a bank card, etc. The idea that you'll need a major credit card to establish credit or pay a bill isn't true. Bills can be paid by bankcards today (your checking account card) or other savvy technological ways as if they *were* actual credit cards. And that's just the way things are *now*. The way technology moves, who knows how easy it will be to make payments and purchases in the future?

When I was younger, a person just about *had* to have at least one major credit card because if you went out of town and for some reason had an emergency that required a large sum of cash quickly, nobody would accept a personal check from your hometown bank (and bank cards weren't available then). Using your credit card was just about the only way to fix your emergency (unless you took large sums of cash along with you). Those days are long gone now. Today's banks are global. Bankcards work just about everywhere. You can *easily* survive without an actual, major credit card. *Easily*.

Unfortunately, most of you won't!

I can hear some of you already ... "Yeah but what about if *I* have an emergency? I don't have extra money in my checking account. I *need* a credit card."

Let me tell you right now, if this is your reasoning for getting a credit card, then this tells me that you haven't planned for your possible emergency very well. Get a savings account for that and put some money in it (now, when you're NOT in an emergency), that requires a 24-hour notice before you can make a withdrawal. This will keep you from being tempted to use it for a quick trip to the local drive-thru and will force you to use your checking account for your emergency. Then, assuming your emergency was legit, you can always take money out of your savings within the next 24 hours and replace the money you withdrew from your checking account.

Besides (and let's be honest here), you and I both know that what most students constitute as an "emergency" compared to an actual emergency, is two different things.

Late-night runs to the local convenience store for cookies, chips, or beer are not "emergencies" as much as I'm sure you're hungry, party-going colleagues will tell you they are!

So play it smart. Keep your own checking and savings accounts and allow your parents or sponsors to deposit money into them on a weekly or monthly basis. But when it comes to credit cards and credit card applications, please heed my advice and just say "NO."

(And please don't be mad at me. I'm serious. I would give just about anything if someone woulda told me this advice when I was younger. You just don't know how serious I am right now.)

P.S. Oh yeah, I almost forgot ... When it comes to the credit card solution (and money matters, too), besides not getting any credit cards, another solution you can do is simply talk to any adults who you believe have made great financial decisions and ask them for advice. Perhaps your parents would be a great source, or maybe they could direct you to people who have been successful in managing money. Just be careful: the people with the biggest house and the fanciest cars aren't always as financially fit as they may seem. Oftentimes they also have the biggest debt, too. Remember ...

It's not about how much someone spends, it's about how much someone keeps.

So find someone who's good at paying their bills on time, keeps their word, isn't too flashy or loud with their money and tends to be ahead of the game. These people may not look the part, but believe me, they tend to have a lot more in their bank account than you'd believe. And it's people like this who seem to have some of the best-kept secrets at holding onto money, while bringing more in.

ATTENTION! Don't know anybody who's been successful with money? No problem! You can also check your local library/book store or even downloadable books online. Many, many books have been written about how to make, save or spend money wisely. So look around. There are plenty of answers right in front of you! And some of them are offered to you for free! ☺

Chapter 29
The Problem with Student Loans

Most of you understand the difference between a loss and a loan, but do you fully grasp what a loan requires? At your age, how many real, actual, interest-bearing loans have you dealt with? Probably little to none. So let me share with you some basics on student loans and how to use them to your advantage.

When it comes to a student loan, it is what it is … a loan for a student. And we all know, if it's a loan, then *ya gotta pay it back!* But do you actually realize that YOU have to pay it back? And not just some of it … ALL OF IT! <u>And with interest</u>!

Loss At First Sight
This might sound like a "duh" moment, but believe me, when you're sitting there filling out the necessary information to apply for student aid, the actual loan concept and the idea of that money still haunting you 10, 15, 20 or MORE years later doesn't quite register at the time.

The excitement of going to college and starting a new chapter in your life, etc., far out-weighs the gravity of exactly what you're agreeing to and exactly how much. At this stage in most college students' lives, the largest loan any of them have ever seen is equal to the amount of money they may have borrowed from a bank or parent to finance the used car they're currently driving, if they're even *that* experienced.

Some students haven't experienced a loan greater than a few bucks here and there borrowed from a friend or relative to cover their high school prom or senior vacation.

Agreeing to a loan of ten, fifteen, or twenty thousand dollars or more (per year!) isn't quite respected for the impact it will hold in your life for the next decade or two (or three, or four).

And how does such a loan affect your college survival?

If you only knew how many students begin college *without* having the end in mind, you'd be amazed. I can't begin to tell you how many students I've known over the years who start off applying and becoming approved for loan after loan to pay their tuition or bills only to find that by the time they get to their senior year (*if* they make it *that* far) they can no longer get approved for any more loans. They've exhausted all their credit! These big-money corporations simply turn them down due to the excessive amount of debt these students have already racked up.

So Close ... And Yet, So Far
What does this mean? This means that unless they can figure out a way to come up with enough money to fund their senior year of college (including living expenses and more) they will be forced to drop out of school temporarily to work or raise more cash. Or worse, drop out of school altogether when they were sooo close to the Finish Line, oftentimes never to return! Now they have a ton of debt, a lifetime of payments ahead of them, and no college degree to show for any of it.

In other words, *they didn't survive.*

So where does this leave you? Does this mean you shouldn't get a student loan? Does it mean you should avoid them altogether and just pay as you go? Perhaps find a smaller school closer to home and work part-time so you can pay your tuition yourself?

These are all good questions and I'll answer them shortly. I will tell you though, whatever you do, **if you heed only one piece of advice out of this entire book, please heed my advice concerning student loans**.

> **If someone (ANYONE!) would've told me what I'm about to share with you, I'd be $60,000 less in debt right now as I currently write this book!**

YES. You read that correctly. **SIXTY-THOUSAND DOLLARS** less!

(Can I say it just one last time? Please? Thanks. Here it goes ... You are sooo lucky to be getting this information *now*. I wish I had this book back then. *You have no idea*. Sigh.)

Okay ... enough of my self-loathing and pity party ... Thanks for indulging me for that brief moment (smile). Now back to helping you survive and live free.

Before I jump to the *My Solution* section and answer several of the questions I mentioned earlier, I need to tell you about one other student loan problem I see often and fell victim to myself. It is the acceptance of student loan excess.

Mo' Money, Mo' Problems

I know of several students who apply for student loans every year and always apply for an amount that is more than (or in excess of) their actual tuition. For example, maybe their tuition for one year will be $12,000, so they apply, qualify, and accept a loan for $15,000. The reasoning for this is that most students believe they need and will use that extra money for "necessary living expenses." Things like food, gas, or maybe even rent (if living off-campus).

Well let me warn you right now ... *this is not a good idea.*

It just adds more money to your debt in the long run, and after you add in interest, that extra $3,000 can cost you more than you ever imagined.

Take may advice. If you must apply for a student loan, do NOT accept more money than your tuition calls for. This extra money rarely gets spent on those "necessary living expenses" (a lot of students just blow it all on clothes, parties, or taking out their friends for fun) and it just adds more debt to the seemingly endless amount you're already racking up. Besides, I've already shown you how to cover those necessary living expenses in Chapter 2, remember? So now you have no excuse!

My Solution

As far as your student loans go, I'm not going to tell you to avoid them (like your credit card applications) but I will tell you to seek EVERY other possible way of getting money for college BEFORE you apply any loans.

For example, one option you have is to apply for a grant. This may be another "duh" moment for some of you, but are you aware that a grant is not the same as a loan? Typically, loans you have to pay back, grants you don't! And grants can be offered for all sorts of reasons. They're not just for those of us that need money for school. You may qualify for a grant for several reasons (household income status, single parent, etc.).

So be sure to look into this option first.[8]

---

[8] Although most grants are given or awarded and are not to be paid back, some may require you to complete a course with certain stipulations (such as a certain G.P.A. or within a specified amount of time,) so be sure to read the fine print! (By the way, did you notice I wrote this section in "fine print" also? I did it to prove my point: if you can read *this* fine print, you can read *anyone's* fine print. So no more excuses!)

Another option to look into before applying for a student loan is scholarships. Do you realize that you don't have to have straight A's or be the most incredible athlete on campus to qualify for a scholarship? Some schools give scholarships for students that can sing, dance, act, play an instrument, and more.

Now you might be saying, "Well that may be true Wilson. And I AM really talented at ____.____ (fill in the blank). But the school I'm going to doesn't give scholarships for this. The school I'm attending only gives academic scholarships and I don't qualify for those. So that won't work for me."

Well if this IS true, then WHY are you going to this college???

(Please read that last line again.)

Why go somewhere that will charge you for your education when you can go somewhere else for free? It doesn't make any sense to me. I realize that students pick colleges for all sorts of reasons, but it really comes down to these basics:

- Does this college offer the major you need for your career?
- Does this college offer you a scholarship for your talent?
- Are you happy here (emotionally, socially, etc.)?
- Can you afford to go here?

And when I say, "Can you afford it?" I don't mean, "Can you get a student loan?" I mean, can you pay for it yourself without getting a loan? If you can't, then I want you to seriously consider the following statement because it could mean the difference between a life of debt or no debt:

> *If you can get the same education (basically) at two different schools and one will pay for some or all of your tuition while the other won't, why pick the one that won't?*

LISTEN TO ME. College will last you roughly 4-6 years depending upon how far you wanna go and how much of my advice in this book you adhere to. But those student loans … *I'm tellin' you* … those things can last for 10, 20, 30 (or more) years!

It's just not worth it.

I've always said, "Go where you're celebrated instead of where you're tolerated." To me, when a college is paying YOU to allow them to educate you, then it sounds like to me they wanna "celebrate you." So let 'em! Opportunities like these don't come around too often. Believe me. So take advantage of them when you can!

Guitar Hero

After writing the previous paragraph, I'm reminded of something that happened to me not too long ago. Allow me to give you the TRUE story of a former student of mine, Jalen.

Jalen was an incredible guitar player. I mean this guy was absolutely amazing. He could play guitar riffs so quickly and clean it was just baffling to watch. He was so impressive to watch that the only thing that amazed me more about Jalen's ability to play the guitar was the fact that he chose to go to a college that doesn't give scholarships for students who do![9]

WHAT? Are you KIDDING ME??? WHY NOT?

Why would he ever go to college and PAY THOUSANDS of dollars (plus interest) for years and years and *years* after he graduates, when he could go to college for FREE??? Well, I asked him. Guess what he said. (You won't believe it.)

He said, "You mean I can get a scholarship that will pay me to go to college just for playing the guitar? I didn't know that."

(If I had a way to insert the sound of a cricket chirping here while all else falls silent wherever you are right now as you read this book I would.)

I just stood there in utter disbelief. Silent. Motionless.

He didn't even know that getting a scholarship for playing the guitar was possible!

What? Seriously??? What is happening here?

How could you have all this talent and go to school from kindergarten to your senior year in high school and *not* know about musical scholarships!!!

Who's guiding this kid?

Where have his parents been? His guidance counselor? Teachers? Me?

UGH! My face cringed.

I was embarrassed and ashamed as an educator and sad for him as well. Here he stands, having made a major financial decision without any educated help or guidance (although it's all around him), that will cost him *thousands and*

---

[9] A college may not have a literal "guitar scholarship" so-to-speak, but many do give scholarships to students who possess a talent or skill (such as playing an instrument) that can be used in the school's band or music department, etc.

thousands of dollars of debt for *years and years* to come, and totally unaware he could've avoided all of it!

And why? Why did he make such a poor decision? Because he simply didn't know any better!

Sad ... just sad.

I could've helped him if he'd only asked. If I'd only known.

He's a casualty to the student loan debt now (like most of us) and he didn't have to be!

But you ...

YOU can avoid this pit! You CAN win! You CAN go to school for FREE (or close to it) and graduate with little or no debt!

All you gotta do is listen to what I'm telling you.

BELIEVE ME, if you have a unique or interesting talent (or even a mediocre one for that matter), if you're a minority, or just academically smart, odds are great that there's a school somewhere that will pay for some or even ALL of your tuition! It's just that easy! All you gotta do is search for them.

Private Investigator

Find a teacher or professor (current or past), a guidance counselor, an older sibling or relative (preferably with a college degree), or some other trusted individual and ask them to help you search for colleges offering scholarships for the specific talent or skill you possess. And don't be too hard on yourself. You may think you don't have a talent or skill worthy of a scholarship but you'd be surprised. There are all types of divisions within the college ranks and all types of colleges.

A Division I school may not offer you anything to play volleyball for them based upon your skill or talent, but a Division II school might think you're amazing and not only offer you a full scholarship to play for them (meaning they'll pay for basically all of your tuition), but even want you be a starter on its team! You never know. *Seriously.*

And just because you may not be an expert in a common sport or musical field, it doesn't mean there isn't a scholarship for you.

Can you bowl?

Shoot a rifle?

Create videos?

Ride a horse?

Paint? Build? Write? Act? Design? Dance? Draw?

The options are seemingly endless. So don't give up too easily. Instead of picking a school and then hoping they have your major and offer a scholarship for it, why not realize what your true talent or skill is first (like I suggested in Chapter 17), and then find a school that will reward you with a free education for it? They're out there and they're looking for someone just like you to come to their campus and make them look good. So why disappoint them?

Find them.

Apply.

Get accepted.

Dominate.

Chapter 30
Is Your School Really Boring? (What To Do)

So you're sooo done with your school. Tired. Bored. And just plain sick of it.

Although I feel for ya, I have a feeling I know why you feel this way. And if I'm right, I believe I can solve your problem without you having to transfer, dropout, or add time to your graduation date.

Wilson, Party Of Four?
I'm reminded of a time when I was out to dinner with a few friends of mine. One of the gentlemen at my table was in charge of a large group of students on his campus and was having a hard time getting them involved in several school activities.

He told me, "These students are so apathetic. They just don't care. I can't get them to do anything, let alone *want* to do anything. What do you suggest?"

As he looked across the table at me sincerely in hopes of a grand answer, I peered just above his shoulder at the waitress cleaning up the table next to him. I told him to turn around and look at her.

I said, "Do you see that waitress over there? She's clearing off the table, removing the used dishes and glasses. Now let me ask you … Does that bother you?"

He looked back at me with a somewhat confused look and said, "No that doesn't bother me. Why should it?"

And I said, "Exactly. It *doesn't* bother you and it *shouldn't*.

Why?

Because those aren't *your* dishes and glasses. You weren't eating off them or drinking from them, so of course it's not going to bother you if the waitress begins to take them away. But what would you do if she came over here right now and began taking away *your* plate, *your* glass, *your* silverware? Imagine if she took it all away right now, without even asking. *Then* how would you feel?"

"Well that would bother me a lot," he said. "I'm not even done eating yet."

This was my point exactly. You see the reason this gentleman's students were so apathetic was because the activities his school and administration had provided for them didn't matter to them. It didn't *involve* them. It wasn't *theirs*.

In the example I'd given him, his school administration played the role of the waitress while his students represented him, the customer. As long as the waitress (the school administration) is messing with dishes from another table (the activities), it's not going to bother the customers (his students) because those dishes aren't *their* dishes.

There is no sense of ownership.

It's the same way with his school's programs. They weren't allowing his students to "own" anything. They weren't permitted to name the programs, have any say in how they operated, let alone run or govern them. They couldn't choose what they wanted out of these programs or how to best implement them in a way that all students would enjoy.

Let me just tell you …

> **There's nothing worse than being involved in an activity, process, or system that has been set-up and constructed by people who aren't the ones who will actually use it.**

Now I'm not suggesting that these kids get to do everything, but the problem was they weren't permitted to do *anything*! All of this was done by his school's staff and administration. I informed him that until he allows his students to play a major role in the construction, programming and implementation of these campus activities, he will find it nearly impossible to get them to participate in any of them, let alone *want* to. If they can't own it, then it's not theirs. If it's not theirs, then why take interest? See what I mean?

Now you may be wondering what all of this ownership has to do with you. I mean sure, you probably get how administration and school faculty would like for you to take interest in their activities, but what exactly does that have to do with you surviving your college experience? Well … to be honest, a lot more than you may think.

Have You Seen My Campus? I Think I Lost It

If you're not interested in what's happening on your campus, then it's less likely it will feel like *your campus.*

The less involved you are with the activities and functions of your school, the more likely it is that you will go home on the weekends (instead of remaining on campus as I've alluded to previously), donate your time and/or energy to things off-campus (which decreases your chances of making new friends, alliances, memories, etc.), and the more likely it is that your college experience won't feel like it's *yours.*

Instead of seeing it as a big part of your life, you'll begin to see it as something that is merely in the way of it. (Yeah … that's another one … read it again).

And when that happens, you know what's next … that old feeling starts creeping in again. You know … the feeling that says, "This college thing just isn't for me. I don't like it here like I thought I would. Maybe this wasn't the right move after all." And the next thing you know you've dropped out of school, returned home to your old world that's comfortable and "safe," and instead of becoming a college graduate, you've become a college casualty.

You'll wake up four or five years from now and realize if you'd stayed in school you would've graduated by now. All of your other friends that went to college (and graduated) now have their degrees and are moving on to their new careers while you're stuck back home doing the same job you were doing before you left, making excuses about why you're not (moving on).

Be honest with yourself now so you don't have to lie to yourself later.

Being involved in on-campus activities and taking ownership in them whenever possible is not only vital to your college survival, but to your future career as well.

Learning how to "own" what you do on a daily basis will help to ensure that you obtain your rightful position in your future career (as well as in life) *and* maintain it as well.

My Solution

If you're going to call your new college residence "home" for the next four years (or more), you might as well run it like it is.

Own the place. Rearrange the furniture. Place your name on the door. Settle in.

You've got to take charge of some things. Make the programs, activities and overall experience your college offers *your* programs, activities and experience.

So get involved. Be a leader.

And if you need help or some ideas on how to do this, just keep reading. The next chapter has some great examples for you to learn from and model! And while you're at it, **make things better than they were before you arrived. Don't wait for your school's faculty or administration to do everything for you**. Unless they're using this book as part of their school curriculum or simply understand such a simple process, they may not even be aware of what they're *not* offering or doing for you.[10]

So don't wait! Part of taking ownership is *taking* ownership. You've got to be assertive (and some times aggressive). Besides, you're the one paying for all of it (whether through time or money or both). And if you're paying for it, then you're buying it. If you're buying it, then it's yours. If it's yours, then own it, personalize it, and put it to work for you.

(Dontchya just love it when I talk to you like I'm your dad? *Smile.* At least you know I care.)

---

[10] Is your high school or college using this book as part of their program or curriculum? If not, please inform them about it and suggest that they implement it in their Freshmen Experience program or something similar.

Chapter 31

How To Make a Grand Exit and Leave a Legacy

One of the best ways to ensure you survive your college experience is by doing something that practically *demands* that you stay at your current school and graduate: Making your mark and leaving your legacy. Both will stay long after you're gone and keep you coming back to ensure that they do. (Your college will LOVE you for this, and you'll love it that much more!)

How do you do it? The trick is to fix something on campus that no one else can fix (or is willing to fix) and then plaster your name all over it (in a very succinct, yet indelible way).

Basically, you find a common but simple problem on campus that garners the attention of students and/or faculty and you solve it in such a way that it not only draws attention to you and your efforts, but also creates a sense of inspiration for others on campus to do the same. Let me give you an example …

There Are No Free Lunches (But What About Free Pencils?)
One year when I was teaching junior high school, I overheard some teachers complaining about several students borrowing their pens and pencils constantly but never returning them. As this group of teachers continued their conversation, several other teachers joined in and complained about how annoyed they were at students borrowing other supplies as well and not returning them.

It seemed to me to be such a trivial thing. I thought to myself, "Is it really *that* bad? All the things that could be wrong in this school and you guys are complaining about pencils and staplers not being returned?"

And then it hit me … It *was* a big deal. It DID matter. It just didn't matter to *me*.

And why? Because those weren't *my* pencils. They weren't *my* staplers.

Ownership kills apathy, remember? Those teachers were upset because *they* were the owners of those pencils. They felt disrespected, unappreciated and taken advantage of. I knew right then if I could find a way to help them feel appreciated and somehow get them some extra pencils and supplies, not only would I solve the problem, but I'd look like a genius doing so.

(Hey … it's the small things in life that count! Remember that.)

So what did I do? I got a large group of students together (roughly 75 total from the seven different classes I taught) and told them about the pencil problem the teachers were having. Besides asking the students to return any pencils they borrow from now on, I also asked each student to bring me two or more packs of new, unused pens and pencils (with at least 10 in each pack), boxes of staples, individual staplers, tape (and other classroom supplies) and a small, home-made card thanking the teachers for their work.

Some students brought in a lot, some brought a little, but all brought some. I then had each student sign their card personally and gathered all the pencils and extra supplies. As my classroom began to fill up with pencils and supplies (and believe me, it did), other students that had originally declined to help now wanted to get in on the event and asked if they could. Of course I let them.

The larger the pile became, the more people wanted to get involved in it. It was contagious! Having more people meant having the ability to do more. So I asked each of the new members to donate $1 or $2 towards a nice, decorative vase. When I had enough money, I purchased several small vases to hold the pens and pencils.

Finally, I printed some elegant name-tag labels from my computer with a description that read, "We love you very much. Thanks for all you do!" And then signed it as being presented by "Mr. Wilson & the junior high students." (Separating my name from the group helped to "brand" my name that much more, thus increasing my popularity with my colleagues and administration.)

I then took each vase and filled it with literally about 40-50 different pens and pencils, and then I slapped that label right on the front of it so everyone could see it. We put the extra supplies in small, decorated shoeboxes that I had my students put together during one of their study halls.

Next, I took my students around the school to each teacher and we "gifted" our vases full of pens and pencils and shoeboxes full of supplies to each of them along with our personal cards.

You should've seen these teachers light up when we did this! They LOVED it!

And why? Was it because they had pens and pencils? No! (Well … maybe just a little.) But more than that, they felt appreciated and heard! They felt deserving of this gift and *they were*. And where do you think each teacher placed that vase? You know exactly where they placed it … right on their desk where everyone could see it.

So what did that mean for my students and me? That meant that all of my colleagues, besides using the free classroom supplies we gave them, were now sitting at their desks using free pens and pencils taken from a beautiful vase with my name right smack dab in the middle of it! In other words, EVERY time any of my colleagues (or student, for that matter) went to grab a pen or pencil from that vase, they saw my name smiling right back at them!

> *Talk about social branding! I practically became everyone's favorite teacher and colleague overnight.*

My name was in every classroom on every teacher's desk and for a good reason. I solved a simple problem with a simple solution and looked like a genius while I did it!

Now you may be saying, "Wilson…that's a great example and all, but that's just pencils … how is that really 'leaving a legacy'?"

Well, to be honest, it's not. But it's the beginning of one. What I've found over the course of my life is that it's far easier to start with what you've got and improve upon it rather than to try to go too big too fast and fail in the process.

You see, what you don't know is, that simple pencil task grew into a much bigger phenomenon. The reaction we got from such a simple thing was sooo strong that I ended up starting a club at school that did nothing but specialize in solving simple but necessary school problems that nobody wanted to solve or had the time to solve (like the pencil problem). We called it an "In-Reach" program (instead of an outreach program) and within a year of the pencil presentation I had an on-campus organization with 118 students as members that met twice a month to gift our school with whatever it needed.

Five years later (Yes, I said FIVE years later) my program had donated thousands of dollars to several businesses and families, including a local church, local college students, and needy families within our school.

We had t-shirts and wristbands and theme songs. We held huge Friday night movie nights and gymnasium parties. We charged $7 total for the entire evening and included food that was donated by local vendors. Having events like this allowed parents to drop off their kids for us to "babysit" while they (the parents) went out on a "date night" without having to take their kids along or pay for an expensive babysitter. Any money we made was used to purchase tools and clothing that we then donated to single moms in our community. We also purchased gift certificates, food, school supplies and more for others.

> *My club even adopted different hallways in our school to keep clean. Instead of "Adopt-a-Highway" we had "Adopt-a-Hallway."*

We also honored individual janitors for their day-to-day efforts as well, awarding them with thank you cards and certificates to nice restaurants.

Let me just tell you, I wasn't playin' around! If you don't think I was well known and liked on that campus after all this you're crazy!

My club name and my own name were on EVERYTHING, EVERYWHERE in that school! It was a beautiful, beautiful thing.

My students loved knowing they were helping others. The teachers loved the gifts they received and the love they felt. And I loved knowing I was a part of something good and gracious.

Everyone won. *Everyone.*

My Solution

If you really need a solution from me after everything I just wrote, you must not be paying attention!

Okay, okay. I'm just givin' you a hard time. But it is true. The stuff I told you about previously is exactly what I did. And doing so allowed me to leave my mark. Not so much on the school (although that's nice, that's really not the goal), but rather, on the hearts of those students and staff members.

Our attitude of giving was contagious. It started a pay-it-forward type of mentality in several of my students that to this day, still contact me and let me know how they are giving and donating to others, long after they've graduated. Seriously. This kind of stuff *really works*. It's the human nature in all of us. But **we started with something small and simple first**. And unless you have a ton of money, power and influence, I recommend you do the same.

I'm a big believer in the K.I.S.S. rule. Ever heard of it?

> *K.I.S.S. (Keep It Simple, Student!)*

You don't have to change the world here, just *yours*.

So keep it simple. Talk with some fellow students. Have a brainstorming session. See what you come up with. Maybe you can get a sponsor for some trees and plant them somewhere on campus that will make a nice place for you and other students to lounge and study on a hot afternoon in the spring.

Or maybe you could raise money to buy a bench or two and place them in some of those super-long hallways in those older buildings on campus. (You know the kind … they look like they were designed in the 1800's and seem to go on forever in one direction.) This would be an easy way to give something practical and useful and still leave your mark. (You can always have one of those small golden plaques put on it that states your name and year donated.)

Becoming Belmont

If you have bigger ideas, you could be like my nephew, Eric. After seeing what his wonderful uncle (me of course!) had been doing all these years, he decided to make HIS mark! While attending Belmont University in Nashville, Tennessee, Eric had become the Student Body President. During this time, he, along with his own college's administration and a local food vendor, generated more than $100,000 in order to have a café built on campus within their school library! Even more, he convinced the school administration to keep the University library open 24 hours/day! This was the first-ever facility on campus to be open 24 hours/day!

Think how useful this was (and still is) to those students there. It was such a big deal that when all of it was completed they even had him join the university president to cut the ribbon on its grand opening!

Talk about BIG! Talk about OWNING THE PLACE! And he managed to do this in only FOUR years while simultaneously graduating as a DOUBLE-MAJOR *and* being in the Honors Program! Yes, that's right. He *earned* TWO bachelor's degrees in only four years while accomplishing this great task! (I'm still impressed to this day!)

And all that work on the café only served to make him *more committed* to his school and graduation. Do you think he was going to go to all that trouble and then drop out or transfer before graduating? NO WAY! **Ownership kills apathy**. *This caused him to be only more committed than ever to his school.*

That's the way to do it. That's how you "own the place." This type of action not only inspires others to do more, but also encourages him to stay in contact with his alma mater and continue to do great things for them as an alumnus. And besides, it looks great on his resume, too!

Some students attend their school. Others *become* their school.

So what about you? What do YOU wanna do? What can you start building, creating, solving?

What Are <u>YOU</u> Becoming?

- *Dartmouth?*
- *NYU?*
- *DePaul?*
- *Oklahoma?*
- *Hawai'i (UH Mānoa)?*
- *San Diego State?*
- *Vanderbilt?*
- *Spelman?*
- *Oxford?*

Columbus State? Boise State? Montana State? ... Notre Dame? Utah? Louisville? ... Morehouse? Otterbein? *Your school???*

What is YOUR school and what do YOU plan to do to leave your mark and make it better?

This is your chance to shine ... a chance to leave a legacy. A chance to exit in grand fashion! We always hear about the "Freshman Experience" but what about the "Senior Experience?" At this level in your collegiate career, this is your chance to make the kind of mark that gives you the opportunity of getting that position, that employment, that place that others only dream of. So whattaya waitin' for? Let's get to it!

Need more ideas? Want some advice? No problem! I'm here to help! Stop by my website (MJ-Wilson.com) or send me an email. I'd love to hear your questions or learn about what you're doing and where. Besides, if you think I'm gonna let my nephew out-do me you're crazy! I'm wanna take this concept global.

So really, send me your questions, ideas and suggestions. As my business grows, I will be "owning the globe" while you "own your school." And who knows? Maybe I'll even come to your school and help you promote your campus-changing project! I'm not kidding ... maybe we could take photos or short video clips and upload them to my site (and your school's) while we challenge other campus organizations, local businesses, or college rivals to do the same!

And just in case you've already started or even completed something major at your school, I'd still like to hear about it! So please email me and let me know what's goin' on. Who knows? Maybe we'll even feature you on our site as well! So send me those pics and tell me those stories! I wanna know what you're up to!

I'm ready. I'm just waitin' on you!

Chapter 32
The Main Reason You Can't Quit

As I sit here and think upon what exactly it is I want to leave you with as I close this book, I am reminded of all the things in life I've always wished someone would've told me "back then" or all the things I wish I'd known then that I know now.

I think about all the times I've said, "If I ever get the chance to speak to the world, even if just for a moment, this is what I'd tell them ..." And now, here I am in my home, sitting at my kitchen table with my computer sorely out of place on top of it, with a cold chill outside on a typical December day in Columbus, Ohio, wondering which of the million things I should share with you at this moment that could change your life for the better.

After much thought, I think I'll leave you with something straight from my heart. Nothin' fancy or pre-made. No clichés or typical texts. Just plain and pure "heart." It may be a little sentimental and perhaps a bit too much for some of you, but I truly believe that what I'm about to share is for somebody out there. Maybe it's for you. Maybe it's not.

Either way, here it is ...

If You Quit, You Lose
When it comes to surviving college, or anything else in life for that matter, it's not so much about what you're facing, as much as it's about how you face it. I know students who have had the greatest odds stacked against them and yet they survived. I also know of students who have had practically everything handed to them, yet they failed.

> *It's never about what life does to us that decides our success, but rather, how we respond to it.*

If you quit, you lose.

If you don't give up, then there's always hope.

When it comes to college, I don't care if you're the first person to go to school from your family and fear you won't survive or if you've quit and returned to school time and time again. I don't care if everyone thinks you're a loser, or stupid, or if nobody believes in you. I don't care if you've been told you'll never make it, or if you've flunked out, gotten pregnant, run out of money, given up, been to prison, believed a lie, or simply just didn't believe you could do it. I'm here to tell you, **you can.**

I believe in you.

I believe you can do it if you **don't quit**.

I *do* care. You *do* matter. You're not stupid. You're not a loser.

You're *human.*

Humans make mistakes. But we learn from them, too. They make us stronger.

Let your mistakes become the roadmap of where you've been and the armor of where you're going.

(Please read that again.)

If anyone can do it, it is those everyone else underestimates. Why? <u>Because we're the least feared and the most dangerous</u>. We've got nothin' to lose and everything to prove.

So don't you quit on me. You hear me?

<u>**DON'T QUIT**</u>.

Hold your head high, show us what you're made of, and make us proud.

Finish school. Get your degree.

And when you do, send me a pic and an email describing your accomplishment. Let me know how you did it and how this book helped. I'd love to hear from you. *Really.* Your stories are what keep me going.

With that, I will close, but in doing so, I want to ask one small favor of you:

Once you have graduated (and I truly mean <u>ONLY</u> after you have graduated!) **would you be so kind as to give this book to someone else that could use it?**

Perhaps a friend, a cousin, a sibling? If this book truly helped you, then this is your chance to truly help someone else. Besides, paying it forward is a beautiful thing that I honestly believe reaps great rewards.

And if for some reason you don't wanna give away your own personal copy (perhaps you marked all through yours or you just want to add it to your personal library) **would you at least consider going to my website and purchasing a new copy or two for someone else?** (Maybe even donate a new copy to your old high school library.) I hate to sound sooo cliché, but together we really can make a difference. *Really*.

So please indulge me if you will and either donate your copy to another future graduate or buy them a new one. I helped you survive, now is your chance to help them!

And speaking of your survival, I wish you the best and look forward to helping you in the future as well – with your employment, relationships, and health. (Hey! You didn't think all I wrote about was education, did you?) Just be sure to check my website occasionally for my future books!

Thanks for listening. And remember, I'll see you at graduation.

-MJ Wilson

You Asked, I Answered

Oftentimes while I'm out on tour speaking at schools and universities, students will pull me aside, or slip me a note and ask me specific questions (usually personal questions) they didn't want to ask publicly. After visiting only a few schools, it didn't take me long to realize that a lot of these questions, although from different students from different schools, were virtually the same.

So I've added *You Asked, I Answered* to this book in hopes of helping those of you out there who may have the same questions (or similar ones) find the answers you need.

So enjoy these questions.[11] And understand that although your situation may be unique to you, most likely somebody somewhere is dealing with or has already dealt with the same thing.

Remember, it's okay to make mistakes … Just make sure they're new ones! Let's learn from others' mistakes, not repeat them!

And please know, I certainly don't know all the details of these situations, **nor do I claim to have all the answers**. I'm simply giving the best advice I can, based upon what little evidence and information I've been given. So indulge me if you will. ☺

---

[11] Student questions have been shortened or paraphrased when and where possible to save time and space.

Can I date my professor?

Dear MJ Wilson,

I am very attracted to my professor and I think he likes me, too. I know it's probably not a good idea, but I was wondering if it would be okay for me to ask him out, after I've finished taking his class. What do you think?

Karen
(Providence, Rhode Island)

- - - - - - -

Dear Karen,

Let me be very clear. You ready? **DO NOT DATE YOUR PROFESSOR**. This is not a smart thing to do while you are a student (even if you are no longer in his class).

First of all, most colleges and universities have rules against anything like this to begin with. So most likely, you run the risk of some type of discipline (possibly even suspension or expulsion) and he runs the risk of losing his job. Even if he doesn't, the integrity of his ability to grade and teach fairly will be seriously hurt, not to mention your own work, especially that which may take place in his class.

If you are seriously interested in this and you believe he is as well, at the minimum I would wait until you were no longer a student at your school or he is no longer a professor there.

Sorry to be so harsh, but it's better for me to be harsh with you now, then the school be harsh with you later, and you not survive college!

Should I get married now?

Dear MJ Wilson,

I have been happily dating the love of my life for more than five years now (we've been together since our sophomore year in high school). I can't imagine myself with anyone else! We're both crazy about each other and I just know we will be married one day. So my question is, do you think it's a good idea for us to get married while I'm still in college? I mean, being together would be so much better than being apart, and I'm sick of living in these dorm rooms! Besides, she has a good paying job and could pay most of our bills while I finish my schooling. What do you think I (we) should do?

Bradley
(Little Rock, Arkansas)

- - - - - - -

Dear Bradley,

I would not get married while still in college. Not because it couldn't work, or because it wouldn't feel right (if she's the love of your life then I'm sure marrying her will be great!) but because marriage is a major, <u>major</u> step in life, and it demands just as much of your time (as college does), if not more.

I've seen many students get married during their college years, and unfortunately, either their schoolwork or their marriage suffers due to the amount of time and energy both demand. In other words, one of them will most likely have to give, and if you wanna save your marriage, most likely it will be your college career.

So if I were you, I'd wait. Your time given to college will most likely be 4-6 years. Your marriage will be forever (hopefully). So **get your degree first.** Besides, if she's the love of your life, she'll not only be there *for* your graduation, but for the rest of your life after!

Should I move out?

Dear MJ Wilson,

I currently live at home with my parents and drive to school each day (it's a community school fewer than 10 minutes away, and it has no dorm rooms or on-campus housing). Recently, one of my friends asked me to move in with her, in a small apartment just off campus. I really wanna move out and get my own place (where I can be treated like an adult). The problem is, if I move in with my friend, I have to pay half the rent, plus utilities. If I stay at home, everything remains free. I'm so unsure of what to do. Please help!

Samantha
(Casper, Wyoming)

— — — — — — —

Dear Samantha,

If I were you I'd stay home … probably. What I mean is, I'm assuming you are under the age of 25 and just feeling a little too "grown" to still be treated like a child. Although this may be true, please remember, FREE is FREE! You have the rest of your life to pay bills and live on your own. Take advantage of this while you can. Eventually you will finish your schooling and then you can pursue your career and your new-found freedom. For now, I'd stay put. (Especially since your school doesn't offer on-campus housing. If it did, and you had a scholarship, I'd recommend you do that instead.)

Since you can't live on campus, I recommend you stay at home and let your parents know (in a very respectful manner) how you feel. You are older. You aren't a child anymore. And technically, if you're 18 years of age or older, you're considered an adult. So perhaps you can have an adult conversation with them and find a happy medium that allows you to stay at home while being treated like the adult you are. (Maybe a later curfew, bigger room, or more privacy. Know what I mean?) Just be sure that if you ask to be treated like an adult, that you act like one. ☺

I would like to say, however, that if you are over 25 years of age and still at home, you may want to consider moving in with your friend, or at the minimum, paying your parents some rent money. By this stage in your life, you should be more than capable of doing one or the other.

Topical Index

ACADEMICS
Grades
18 – Why Grades Matter
114 – Why Grades Don't Matter

Exams/Tests
43 – How To Deal With Test Stress
84 – Bad Professors, Impossible Exams
89 – How To Study For And Pass Impossible Exams

Also See **Professors**

ALCOHOL
63 – Parties, Alcohol And Sex: Everyone's Doing It ... Should I?
65 – Statistics
65 – Underage Drinking
65 – Fake ID's
66 – Driving Under The Influence (DUI)

BOREDOM
See **Campus Culture**

CAMPUS CULTURE
14 – Dating And Social Status
16 – Religious Beliefs And Parties
18 – Clubs, Sports And Academics
19 – Traditions
22 – Campus Personality (The Campus's Cultural Atmosphere)
136 – How Not Knowing Your School's Traditions Affects Your Graduation Chances
154 – Boredom/Getting Involved

TRADITIONS

Also See **Hazing**

TRANSFERRING SCHOOLS

TRANSPORTATION

VISION

WEIGHT

See **Health**

College Index

The following is a list of all the colleges mentioned throughout this book:

*We avoided using numbered references throughout this text in an effort to create a book that flows easily for the reader, without feeling too academic or scientific in its approach. However, we feel it is important that you (students, parents and school administrators) know *some* of our sources (there were just too many to list!) and, should you wish to read more about non-academic barriers to college student success (and their related topics), have access to several of the articles and textbooks we used in our research. ☺

-MJ Wilson / Dr. JoNataye

Research/Chapter Notes*

Chapter 1 – The First Month of School

1. Pritchard, M. E., Wilson, G.S., &Yamnitz, B. (2007). What predicts adjustment among college students? A longitudinal panel study. *Journal of American College Health, 56*(1), 15-22.
2. McLeod, W.B., & Young, J.M. (2005). A chancellor's vision: Establishing an institutional culture of student success. *New Directions for Institutional Research, 125,* 3-85.
3. Allen-Collinson, J., & Brown, R. (2012). I'm reddie and a Christian! Identity negotiations amongst first year university students. *Studies in Higher Education, 37*(4), 497-51.
4. Basset, J., & Snyder, T.L. (2013). "Parenting" in the classroom: University students' evaluation of hypothetical instructors as a function of teaching styles and "parenting" styles. *North American Journal of Psychology, 15*(3), 447-462.
5. Crede, M., & Niehorster, S. (2012). Adjustment to college as measured by the student adaptation to college questionnaire: A qualitative review of its structure and relationships with correlates and consequences. *Educational Psychology Review, 24*(1), 133-165.
6. Thompson, L. J., Clark, G., Walker, M., & Whyatt, J.D. (2013). 'It's just like an extra string to your bow': Exploring higher education students' perceptions and experiences of extracurricular activity and employability. *Active Learning in Higher Education, 14* (2), 135-147.
7. Muldoon, R. (2009). Recognizing the enhancement of graduate attributes and employability through part-time work while at university. *Active Learning in Higher Education, 10* (3), 237-252.

Chapter 2 – College Life – The Pressure To Fit In

1. Chock, T., M., Wolf, J.M. Chen, G.M., Schweisberger, V.N., & Yi, W. (2013). Social media features attract college students to news websites. *Newspaper Research Journal, 34* (4), 96-108.
2. Luyckx, K., Klimstra, T.A., Duriez, B., Petegem, S.V., Beyers, W., Teppers, E., & Goossens, L. (2013). Personal identity processes and self-esteem: Temporal sequences in high school and college students. *Journal of Research in Personality, 47* (2), 159-170.
3. Downey, C.A., & Chang, E.C. (2013). Assessment of everyday beliefs about health: The lay concepts of health Inventory, college student version. *Psychology & Health. 28*(7), 818-832.

Chapter 3 – Are You Homesick or Lovesick?

1. Woosley, S.A, & Shepler, D.K. (2011). Understanding the early integration experiences of first-generation college students. *College Student Journal, 45*(4), 700-714.
2. Rose, S. (2013). The value of a college degree. *Change, 45*(6), 24-33.
3. Thurber, C.A., & Walton, E. (2012). Homesickness and adjustment in university students. Journal of American *College Health, 60*(5), 415-419.
4. United States Census Bureau. (2014, February 24). *Education: Higher Education: Degrees.*
   Retrieved from:
   http://www.census.gov/compendia/statab/cats/education/higher_education_degrees.html
5. Ramsey, M.A., Gentzler, A. L., Morey, J.N., Oberhauser, A.M., & Westerman, D. (2012). College students' use of communication technology with parents: Comparisons between two cohorts in 2009 and 2011. *CyberPsychology, Behavior & Social Networking, 16* (10), 747-752.
6. Kinney, A. (2010). When distance is problematic: Communication, coping, and relational satisfaction in female college students' long-distance dating relationships**.** *Journal of Applied Communication Research, 38* (1), 27-46.

Chapter 4 – What To Do When Nobody Knows Who You Are

Mendoza, P., Horton, D., & Mendez, J.P. (2012). Retention among community college student-athletes. *Community College Journal of Research & Practice, 36*(3), 201-219.

Chapter 5 – How To Deal with Test Stress

Ying, L., & Lindsey, B. (2013). An association between college students' health promotion practices and perceived stress. *College Student Journal, 47,* 437-446.

Chapter 6 – Everyday Problems All College Students Face

1. McKinley, C. (2013). Applying a distress-deterring approach to examine how emotional support predicts perceived stress and stress-related coping response. *Southern Communication Journal, 78*(5), 387-404.
2. Thurber, C.A., & Walton, E.A. (2012). Homesickness and adjustment in university students. *Journal of American College Health, 60*(5), 415-419.
3. Pittman, L.D., & Richmond, A. (2008). University belonging, friendship quality, and psychological adjustment during the transition to college. *Journal of Experimental Education, 76*(4), 343-362.

Chapter 7 – So You Think You Need a Car?

Goldstein, S.B. (2013). Predicting college students' intergroup friendships across race/ethnicity, religion, sexual orientation, and social class. *Equity & Excellence in Education, 46*(4), 502-519.

Chapter 8 – So You Think You Need a Job?

1. Chaun, S.F., Chau, A.W., & Chan, K.Y. (2012). Financial knowledge and aptitudes: Impacts on college students' financial well-being. *College Student Journal, 46*(1), 114-132.
2. Hall, R. (2010). The work-study relationship: Experiences of full-time university students undertaking part-time employment. *Journal of Education & Work, 23*(5), 439-449.

Chapter 9 – The Super Friends

Pittman, L.D., & Richmond, A. (2008). University belonging, friendship quality, and psychological adjustment during the transition to college. *Journal of Experimental Education, 76*(4), 343-362.

Chapter 10 – Old Friends vs. New Friends

1. Steams, E., Buchman, C., & Bonneau, K. (2009). Interracial friendships in the transition to college. Do birds of a feather flock together once they leave the nest? *Sociology of Education, 82*(2), 173-195.
2. Maunder, R., Cunliffe, M., Galvin, J., Mjali, S., & Rogers, J. (2013). Listening to student voices: Student researchers exploring undergraduate experiences of university transition. *Higher Education, 66*(2), 139-152.

Chapter 11 – Parties, Alcohol and Sex

1. Trieu, S.L., Shenoy, D.P., Braftton, S., & Marshak, H.H. (2011). Provision of emergency contraception at student health centers in California community colleges. *Women's Health, 21*(6), 431-437.
2. Allen-Collinson, J., & Brown, R. (2012). I'm a reddie and a Christian! Identity negotiations amongst first-year university students. *Studies in Higher Education, 37*(4), 497-511.
3. Nguyen, N., Walters, S.T., Wyatt, T.M., & DeJong, W. (2013). Do college drinkers learn from their mistakes recent alcohol-related consequences on planned protective drinking strategies among college freshman. *Substance Use & Misuse, 48*(14), 1463-1468.
4. Toews, M.L., & Yazedijan, A. (2012). College students' knowledge, attitudes, and behaviors regarding sex and contraceptives. *Journal of Family and Consumer Sciences, 104*(3), 16-23.

Chapter 12 – The Problem with Hazing

Hollman, B.B. (2002). Hazing: Hitting campus crime. *New Directions for Student Services, 99,* 11-23.

Chapter 13 – On-Campus Clubs: Should You Join Them?

1. Asel, A.M., Seifert, T.A. & Pascarella, E.T. (2009). The effects of fraternity/sorority membership on college experiences and outcomes: A portrait of complexity. Oracle: *The Research Journal of the Association of Fraternity/Sorority Advisors, 4*(2), 1-15.

2. Powell, P.W., Gray, G., & Reese, M.K. (2013). Connecting with others: A qualitative study of online social networking site usage. *Practitioner Scholar: Journal of Counseling and Professional Psychology, 2*(1), 52-67.

Chapter 14 – Why You Definitely Need a College Roadmap
1. Coretez, L.J. (2011). A roadmap to their future: What Latino students need to graduate. *Chronicle of Higher Education, 58*(6), B21-B25.
2. Acee, T. W., Cho, Y., Kim, J., & Weinstein, C.E. (2012). Relationships among properties of college students' self-centered academic goals and academic achievement. *Educational Psychology, 32*(6), 681-698.

Chapter 15 – How To Find Good Professors
1. Strage, A. (2008). Traditional and non-traditional college students' descriptions of the "ideal" professor and the "ideal" course and perceived strengths and limitations. *College Student Journal, 42*(1), 225-231.
2. Griffin, K.A., (2012). Learning to mentor: A mixed methods study of the nature and influence of Black professors' socialization into their roles as mentors. *Journal of the Professoriate, 6*(2), 27-58.
3. Roshethal, K., & Shinebarger, S.H. (2010). In practice: Peer mentors: Helping bridge the advising gap. *About Campus, 15*(1), 24-27.

Chapter 16 – Bad Professors/Impossible Exams (What To Do)
1. Holland, N.E. (2011). The power of peers: Influences on postsecondary education planning and experiences of African American students. *Urban Education, 46*(5), 1029-1055.
2. Gordon-Hickey, S., & Lemley, T. (2012). Background noise acceptance and personality factors involved in library environment choices by college students. *Journal of Academic Librarianship, 38*(6), 365-369.
3. Strayhorn, T. L. (2011). Bridging the pipeline: Increasing underrepresented students' preparation for college through a summer bridge program. *American Behavioral Scientist, 55*(2), 142-159.

Chapter 17 – How To Choose the Right Major
1. Zafar, B. (2012). Double majors: One for me, one for the parents? *Economic Inquiry, 50*(2), 287-308.
2. Adams, C.J. (2013). Choosing a college. *Education Week, 33*(4) 5.
3. May, R. W., & Cassazza, S.P. (2012). Academic major as a perceived stress indicator: Extending stress management intervention. *College Student Journal, 46*(2), 264-273.

Chapter 18 – Is It Okay To Change Your Major?
1. Walker, L.H.M., & Sted, M. (2013). Integrating identities: Ethnic and academic identities among diverse college students. *Teachers College Record, 115*(8), 1-24.
2. Visher, M.G., & Bhandari, R.M.E. (2004). High school career exploration programs: Do they work? *Phi Delta Kappan, 86*(2), 135-138.

Chapter 19 – Is It Bad To Transfer to Another School?
1. Carter, C. (2007). Top 10 reasons students struggle and drop out freshmen year – and what you can do about it. *Recruitment and Retention in Higher Education, 21*(7), 33-5.

2.   Barefoot, B.O. (2004). Higher education's revolving door: Confronting the problem of student dropout in US colleges and universities. *Open Learning, 19*(1), 9-19.

3.   McMullin, K. (2012). College visits should be fun, not stressful, *Careers & Colleges,* 18-19.

Chapter 20 – How Important Are Your Grades?

Firmin, M.W., & Krista, M. (2007). Driven and no regrets: A qualitative analysis of students earning baccalaureate degrees in three years. *Education Research Quarterly, 31*(2), 30-43.

Chapter 21 – The Freshman 15 (Are You Gaining Weight?)

1.   Carithers-Thomas, J.A., Bradford, S.H., Keshock, C.M, & Pugh, S. F., (2010). Freshman Fifteen: Fact or fiction? *College Student Journal, 44*(2), 419-423.

2.   Largo-Wight, E., Peterson, P., & Michael, C.W. (2005). Perceived problem solving, stress, and health among college students. *American Journal of Health Behavior, 29*(4), 360-370.

3.   Obesity Hotline http://obesityhotline.com/

Chapter 22 – Are You Thinking of Dropping Out?

1.   Doubleday, J. (2013). Narrowing gaps, but a diploma still pays, report says. *Chronicle of Higher Education, 60*(7), A14.

2.   Gilardi, S., & Guglielmetti, C. (2001), University life of non-traditional students: Engagement styles and impact on attrition. *Journal of Higher Education, 82*(1), 33-53.

Chapter 23 – What You Should Be Doing on the Weekends

1.   Thompson, L.J., Clark, G.W., Walker, M., & Whyatt, J.D. (2013)."It's just like an extra string to your bow': Exploring higher education students' perceptions and experiences of extracurricular activity and employability. *Active Learning in Higher Education, 14*(2), 135-147.

2.   Wohn, D.Y., Ellison, N.B., Khan, ML., Fewins-Bliss, R., & Gray, R. (2013). The role of social media in shaping first-generation high school students' college aspirations: A social capital lens. *Computers & Education, 63*, 424-436.

Chapter 24 – Why Your Dorm Room Needs Help

1.   Bennett, C., Jane, J. (200). Cool for school. *Kiplinger's Personal Finance, 54*(8), 156.

2.   Farber, N., (2012, May 22). *Throw away your vision board: Vision boards are for dreaming, action boards are for achieving.* Psychology Today. Retrieved from: http://www.psychologytoday.com/blog/the-blame-game/201205/throw-away-your-vision-board-0

Chapter 25 – The Problem with Your College Clothing

The School Spirit Study Group (2004). Measuring school spirit: A national teaching exercise. *Teaching of Psychology, 31*(1), 18-21.

Chapter 26 – The "Stagnation after Graduation" Problem

Kiefer, H.M. (2005, June, 14). *High school: Worst of times or best of times? Most wish they'd hit the books a little harder.* Gallup. Retrieved from: http://www.gallup.com/poll/16807/high-school-worst-times-best-times.aspx

Chapter 27 – Great Stuff You're Missing on Your Own Campus

1. Buckeyefansonly.com. (2014, February 24). *Football Traditions.* Retrieved from: http://buckeyefansonly.com/traditions.html
2. Jackson, J.W, Miller, D.A., Frew, E.J., Gilbreath, B. & Dillman, C. (2011). Group identification and university involvement. *Journal of Applied Social Psychology, 41*(4), 798-822.
3. Yin, D., & Lei, S.A. (2007). Impacts of campus involvement on hospitality student achievement and satisfaction, *Education, 128*(2), 282-293.

Chapter 28 – The Problem with College Credit Cards

1. Hawkins, J. (2012). The CARD act on campus. *Washington, & Lee Law Review, 69*(3), 1471-1534.
2. Hogan, E. A., & Bryant, S.K. (2013). Relationships between college students' credit card debt, undesirable academic behaviors and cognitions, and academic performance. *College Student Journal, 47*(1), 102-112.
3. Nance-Nash, S. (2012). Planning my financial future. *Black Enterprise*, 63-64.

Chapter 29 – The Problem with Student Loans

1. Wenisch, M. (2012). The student loan crisis and the future of higher education. *Social Science Review, 17*, 345-350.
2. Federal Student Aid and Office of the U.S. Department of Education. (2014, February 24). *Grants and scholarships are free money to help pay for college or career school.* Retrieved from: http://studentaid.ed.gov/types/grants-scholarships
3. FastWeb.com Web site: http://www.fastweb.com
4. Scholarships.com (2014, February 24). *Music scholarships.* Retrieved from: https://www.scholarships.com/

Chapter 30 – Is Your School Really Boring? (What To Do)

Walsh, M. (2009). Students shaping dialogue about college events: Ideas for academic engagement. *College Student Journal, 43*(1), 216 – 220.

Chapter 31 – How To Make a Grand Exit and Leave a Legacy

Wang, T.R. (2012). Understanding the memorable messages first-generation college students receive from on-campus mentors. *Communication Education, 61*(4), 353-357.

Chapter 32 – The Main Reason You Can't Quit

Jackson, R., Weiss, K.E., Lundquist, J.J., & Hooper, D. (2003). The impact of hope, procrastination, and social activity on academic performance of Midwestern college students. *Education, 124*(2), 310-320.

Acknowledgments -MJ Wilson

Much of the success I have today in my speaking and writing career is in large part due to the people and organizations I've met along the way. These people and organizations were either major turning points in my educational career, or they encouraged me to become so much more than what I was. And some are the reason I am able to write such a rich, authentic, practical book today.

So with that being said, and in no particular order, let's get started ...

Fred Reeder (OnCampusSports.com) – You've been my best friend since the 5th grade. You've known me through practically every stage of my life. Friends like you are *rare*. Your input, heart and genuine goodness is lacking greatly in this world today. My world is better because you have remained in it. I am grateful for your grammar expertise (who else would edit this book for free?) and your advice, but mostly your friendship. You (and your family) have always treated me with such dignity and respect over the years and it has meant so much to me. *I have no doubt this book will go far beyond anything I could've ever imagined, simply because of your input and direction*. I am truly, truly thankful. Here's to many more years to come!

Steve J. Vekich (my former professor at Washington State Community College, Marietta, Ohio) – If it weren't for you, I'd still be working at Sears in Parkersburg, WV, dreaming of becoming an educator. YOU made a HUGE difference in my life and career as a teacher. You were the first professor I had that I felt truly saw more in your students than we did in ourselves. Rarely do people and opportunities like you come along. To say that I am grateful would be an understatement. *I am honored*. Thank you for believing in me when I didn't believe in myself. You have my undying respect. If I'm only half the educator you are and have been, I am light years ahead of the rest.

Rick Boothby (my former music professor at Ohio Valley University, Parkersburg, WV) – Thank you for getting *real* with me and telling me exactly what I needed to hear at just the right time. I'll never forget the day you walked into my job and ever-so-skeptically asked, "Wilson ... What are you doing here? Why didn't you finish your degree?" You gave me a chance to go back to school and made me feel at home when I did. The memories we created singing in the A Cappella Singers and traveling on tour are priceless. *Your honesty and friendship have never been forgotten, and never will*. Thank you for expecting more from me than I did from myself. I am on a better path in life because of you.

John Gibson (friend, supporter, and former colleague) – After teaching alongside you for eight years, I must say, I learned quite a bit from you. Your ability to tell a story, capture an audience, intrigue the listener, and tug at the heart is nothing short of amazing. I would often observe how you would move throughout a room and manage to evoke the right emotion at the right time during any speech. I am so blessed to have met you and have the privilege to not only learn with you, but learn from you. Your friendship and genuine kindness that you (and your family) have shown me over the years are heartfelt to this day. Thank you for helping, teaching and guiding me. I'm a better instructor and speaker because of you.

Dr. JoNataye Prather (DrJoNataye.com) – Oh the day that I met you ... you made me so envious! Here I was bragging about the possibility of going back to school to get my Master's and you already had yours and were working on your PhD! I felt so humbled, so fast! I had to step back for a minute and take in exactly who you were and what you were all about. You are not only an inspiration to people wherever you go, but a great challenger as well. You have challenged me to be so much more than I originally planned, and I'm so appreciative. I look forward to many, many successful years working with you, and especially our first conference in Dubai! *Thank you for all your help and research with this book specifically*, and my career. It means a lot to me.

Mr. Jeff Clark (Lakeview Junior High principal) – Wow! You are one of the most amazing principals ever! Talk about understanding leadership! *Pickerington would not be the same without you.* Working at your school and under your leadership gave me hope that all in the education world has not been lost! YES. There STILL ARE principals who have a backbone, who lead by example, who defend their staff, and discipline them when needed. Principals who remember why they got in this thing called education to begin with. People like you restore what's lacking in administration today: PRIDE. Thank you for being such a great role model as an educator and leader. But most of all, thank you for actually taking responsibility for the position you hold in so many lives. You don't just set the example, you *are* the example.

Dr. Virginia LeBlanc (TheLeBlancGroupOnline.com) – You are a true entrepreneur and visionary! If I had half your energy ... I can only imagine what I would accomplish. Thank you for your support and promotion of my career and vision. You believed in me and heard me when I wasn't even sure I was hearing myself. Your willingness to go for your dream has inspired me to continue to go for mine. *Thank you for raising the bar.* I strive harder because of you. You have been, and continue to be, a blessing.

Otterbein University (Westerville, Ohio) – My alma mater. I had a *phenomenal* experience while attending grad school here. Beautiful campus, caring professors, insightful classes. Such a great, <u>great</u> university. I love the fact that you have managed to stay current with education while maintaining a respect for the past. The vibe and energy I felt while on campus here was so pure, so true, and so *academic*. I loved my time here, and can't wait to return to speak, share, and yes, learn. What a great, great school.

Dr. Wendy Sherman-Heckler (one of my former professors at Otterbein University) – Of all the professors I've had, you are one of the few who taught the student every bit as much as you taught the subject. I truly appreciate your ability to understand *who* you're teaching as much as *what* you're teaching. I didn't just attend your classes, I *learned* in them. You are a great professor, and your merit and candor do not go unnoticed. Thank you for educating me.

Dr. Daniel Cho (another former professor of mine, Otterbein University) – You are one of my all-time <u>favorite</u> professors! You are the only guy I know who can spar with me on any topic and win more often than you lose! *What an innovative thinker you are.* Your ability to see things from an angle most people don't even realize exists is amazing. You have truly opened my eyes and mind to things that were right in front of me, yet I never saw. I am a better thinker, listener, philosopher, teacher, and most importantly, student, because of you. Thank you for challenging my beliefs and perceptions, and my sense of reason. *I believe you are one of the greatest teachers of all time because you are one of the greatest learners of all time.* Thank you, sir. Thank you.

Kim Love (friend and major supporter) – You may have been the very first person to actually call me "Doc." Your encouragement to me over the years to pursue my career was (and still is) very needed. I remember you asking me for advice one morning in my classroom before school started and how impressed you were with my answer. You told me, "Doc … You need to be sharing this stuff with the world. People need to hear this." It was <u>then</u> that I realized how necessary it was for me to start writing. Not just educational books, but relationship books, too. Your support and insight about me has been a major cultivation of my gift as a writer and thinker, and I am grateful. *Thank you.*

Dave & Jackie Dorman – Plain and simple: Good People. Seriously. Every time I think of you two, that is the phrase that comes to mind … Good People. The support you both have given me over the past few years has been so encouraging and so needed. I lost a few friends on this journey simply for following my dreams. But you guys … When others thought I was crazy for pursuing this career, you only drew closer to me. You not only encouraged me to believe in my dreams, but you showed me how. Your example of passion and commitment to a cause is like none other. And your willingness to promote me (and my book) has been so, so helpful. Just know that I believe in you as much as you both believe in me. And I love you with all my heart.

The following people and organizations have been instrumental in making my "MJ Wilson" brand a reality. Without their support, this entire process would have taken so much longer:

Ohio Dominican University (Columbus, Ohio) – YOU were one of the first universities to take me in and allow me to speak when I was virtually unknown and didn't have a book, website, or a ton of references to speak of. (So glad those days are behind us!) Thank you for taking a chance on me and allowing me the privilege of speaking to your wonderful students and staff. I appreciate your support – especially since you gave it to me when no one else would or could. Much respect to you.

Indiana University (Bloomington, Indiana) – Of all the places I've been invited to speak, IU is definitely one of my favorites! So welcoming and so willing to help! I remember speaking at the HHSP event back in 2011 … What a great group of people and such a great time. I was (and still am) impressed with your school's (and program's) desire to bring people together of different races, ethnicities, religions, and cultures, all for a greater cause and understanding. *That is rare today.* I was so honored to be a part of that event (and hope to do so again, someday … hint hint!) Thanks again. I will see you soon!

Dr. Miriam "Mimi" Attenoukon (Indiana University) – Ahhh Mimi … By far the sweetest, kindest voice I've ever heard on the other end of a business call. Your patience and willingness to work with me (and I'm sure with others) does not go unnoticed. Keep doing what you're doing. The educational field needs more people like you! (Do you still have the picture I sent you? I still have mine!) Never, NEVER stop doing what you do! IU is a better place because of you, and your passion to help others is contagious!

Anthony Scott, J.D. (Herron School of Art and Design at IUPUI) – Thank you for allowing me to be a part of your HHSP program while at Indiana University and for the kind words you spoke while I was there. It was such a privilege to be a part of what you were doing. Your story is inspiring and *your support of me then has been of great benefit to me now.* I hope to visit your new school soon and return the favor!

Kirsten & Kyle Moses (keekcreative.com) – You two are some of the best designers on this planet! What you did with my website, logo, business cards, book cover and more is simply amazing! I never cease to be in awe of your creativity. I am so thankful for your input, your patience, and most importantly, your love. Kirsten, I am so proud to have you as my niece, and Kyle, as one of my former students, I can't think of any other man I'd be happier to see with her! I love you both dearly. Thank you.

Additional Thanks:

I'd like to thank my sister, **Kelita Deems**, for her patience while helping me structure this book *and* for being so willing to be my "free secretary." (At least for now!)

I'd like to thank **Linda "Toya" Topping** for reading over the rough drafts and giving me feedback. The perception and opinions provided were very useful and certainly added to the expertise of this book.

I'd like to thank **Samantha Davis** for the additional research, clerical support and educational expertise concerning this project.

Finally, I'd like to thank **my parents**, both of which are some of the greatest supporters and promoters I know. People say, "You can never repay your parents for all they do." That may be true, but I'm sure gonna try! I love you both!

If I've forgotten anyone, I do apologize. You know who you are! Thank you!

About The Author
MJ Wilson

MJ Wilson is an educator, author and speaker.

EXPERIENCE
With more than 15 years' experience in the teaching profession, he is no stranger to the classroom. Wilson has taught at each grade level from 5th through 12th and has instructed more than 1,500 students during the span of his career. This includes teaching in urban and rural schools, public and private, and spending two years as a substitute teacher (during which he often claims he learned as much as he taught!)

EDUCATION
MJ Wilson obtained his Bachelor of Science degree (with an emphasis in Elementary Education) from Ohio Valley University (Parkersburg, WV) in 1998.

Wilson currently holds a Master of Arts in Education degree (with an emphasis in Curriculum & Instruction), which he obtained from Otterbein University (Westerville, Ohio) in 2010.*

*Capstone Project: *Self Study: An Exploration Of What I Learned From Educators' Perceptions Of Non-Academic Obstacles To At-Risk Students*

CAREER
MJ Wilson is an author of other books as well (mainly dealing with motivation and relationships) and has several slated for release in the very near future. (Feel free to check his website frequently to view/purchase his latest project!)

PERSONAL NOTES
A strong believer in keeping a healthy mind and body, Wilson can often be found at the local gym near his home, where he is not only a member, but also a certified fitness instructor, teaching a variety of cardio fit classes each month.

In his spare time (which according to him is "rare"), he enjoys outdoor activities, anything dealing with anthropology, and traveling the globe experiencing new foods and cultures.

Wilson resides in Columbus, Ohio, where he writes, educates and dreams.

For more information about MJ Wilson as an author and speaker, you can follow him on Twitter (***@AuthorMJWilson***) or visit his website.

MJ-Wilson.com

About The Researcher
JoNataye Prather

Dr. JoNataye Prather is a nationally recognized educator, consultant and speaker.

EXPERIENCE
As an educator for more than 15 years, her past experience includes working as a school social worker and consultant while completing research as a teaching assistant at The Ohio State University. Currently, she educates and inspires students as an assistant professor and Field Director of Social Work at Ohio Dominican University (Columbus, OH).

Dr. JoNataye has presented at national conferences, as well as colleges and universities, advising about non-academic barriers to learning. Her methods involve enhanced student matriculation, professional development and increased personal growth.

EDUCATION
Dr. JoNataye received all three of her degrees from The Ohio State University.
-Bachelor of Arts in Psychology and African-American Studies (1999)
-Master's in Social Work (2001)
-PhD (2010)*

*Dissertation Research: *A View from the Principal's Office: A Grounded-Theory Exploration of Principals' Perceptions of Non-Academic Barriers to Learning*

CAREER
Loaded with a bounty of research and practical solutions, Dr. JoNataye often works with businesses and non-profit organizations to promote a positive workplace climate. Students, educators and human service practitioners nationwide have benefited from her insightfulness, compassion and spirit of enthusiasm to transform their organization and personal lives.

PERSONAL NOTES
Dr. JoNataye currently resides in Columbus, Ohio, where she is developing several educational tools to help graduates pursue their PhD in a timely, practical fashion.

For more information about Dr. JoNataye as a consultant or speaker, you can follow her on Twitter (***@DrJoNataye***) or visit her website.

DrJoNataye.com